ADVANCED
CROSS COUNTRY
RIDING

HOW TO SUCCEED IN HORSE TRIALS

ADVANCED CROSS COUNTRY RIDING

HOW TO SUCCEED IN HORSE TRIALS

JANE HOLDERNESS-RODDAM

Photography by
BOB LANGRISH

WARD LOCK

TITLE PAGE *Mary Thomson still manages a smile after bouncing into the lake on King Boris. However, his head is still down and Mary is trying her utmost to stay in the middle.*

A WARD LOCK BOOK

First published in the UK 1994
by Ward Lock
Villiers House
41/47 Strand
LONDON
WC2N 5JE
A Cassell Imprint
Copyright © Ward Lock 1994

Distributed in the United States
by Sterling Publishing Co., Inc.
387 Park Avenue South, New York, NY 10016-8810

Distributed in Australia
by Capricorn Link (Australia) Pty Ltd
2/13 Carrington Road, Castle Hill, NSW 2154

A British Library Cataloguing in Publication Data block for this book
may be obtained from the British Library

ISBN 0-7063-7164-X

Typeset by Litho Link Ltd, Welshpool, Powys, Wales
Printed and bound in Great Britain by The Bath Press, Avon

CONTENTS

INTRODUCTION   7

1 THE BASIC REQUIREMENTS OF HORSE AND RIDER   8

2 STABLE MANAGEMENT   31

3 DEVELOPING FITNESS   54

4 POLE WORK AND JUMP TRAINING   85

5 FAST WORK, GROUND CONDITIONS AND THE WEATHER   128

6 COMPETING AT EVENTS   145

INDEX   175

ACKNOWLEDGEMENTS

The author would like to thank all those who helped towards the publication of this book, particularly Bob Langrish for his excellent photographs and Sandra McCallum for typing the manuscript. Also Franziska Lewinski and Darrell Scaife who helped with the photography at Mr and Mrs Sanderson's Fern Farm cross country schooling course near Swindon.

INTRODUCTION

Nothing is more exciting or exhilarating than riding over big fences across country on a bold horse. Having been lucky enough to have ridden round some of the world's greatest three-day events on various horses over the last 25 years, I have experienced many memorable moments that have stirred almost every emotion possible: fear, excitement, anticipation, pride, gratitude and, perhaps more than anything, humility when it has been the generous and bold nature, plus the sheer power, of my horse which, time and again, has rescued me from a seemingly impossible situation.

Perhaps the very nature of the sport of eventing and riding across country brings out the best in both humans and equines. The unpredictability of it all and that fine line that lies between success and failure help to create a unique understanding, not only between horse and rider but also among fellow competitors. Other riders are always very understanding when things go wrong and so willing to help or offer advice if it is needed as, without exception, we have all experienced the bad times as well as the good.

In this book, I hope I can offer some useful tips to anyone wanting to compete seriously. Along the way I have learnt a great deal from watching, listening and, of course, competing, which might help others to experience some of the fun and, I hope, success that I have been able to enjoy over the years.

The Basic Requirements of Horse and Rider

Riding across country is a thrilling experience, and never more so than when horse and rider are moving in complete harmony, jumping each and every fence with confidence and ease. To achieve this, however, takes years of experience and many months of hard work to produce a horse that is fit, willing and able to cope with the demands involved.

Numerous different factors come into play when one is setting out to train a cross country horse, not least the rider's mental approach to this preparation. Other points include the horse's conformation and how this might affect its ability or suitability for cross country work, in particular, how its limbs and feet are formed, its general action and way of going. The importance of correct shoeing and basic leg care, throughout its entire career, cannot be overemphasized. It is also vital for the rider to establish a good rapport with, and thorough understanding of, the horse, its temperament and how to get the best out of it if its true potential is to be realized, therefore a certain amount of knowledge of the psychology of the horse is necessary. Sound stable management and the ability to notice problems before they become serious also play a big part in creating success.

THOROUGH PREPARATION

A clear-cut programme must be set for each and every horse, which should take into account such things as its age and experience, temperament, mental and physical development, whether or not it has had a trouble-free build-up to its present condition, how thorough and how advanced its training has been to date, whether it has natural or average ability, whether it is good, bad or exceptional, both on the flat and over fences, and whether it seems tough and able to stand up to the demands of what is, without doubt, a strenuous and rugged sport.

Once these considerations have been thoroughly examined, a programme can be arranged to suit each particular horse in order to bring out the very best in it through careful training and a structured, but flexible, schedule. So often, young horses are pushed on too quickly and ruined before their true potential is ever realized. It is, therefore, particularly important that a realistic programme is established in the first place. If the horse progresses quickly and without problems, there is still always the risk of asking too much just once too often, so do set a cut-off point, designed to give the horse a rest, both mental and physical, to ensure that this does not happen. Later, you can start again and, this time, go a little further if the horse continues to progress satisfactorily.

If problems are encountered, work out why they have arisen and go back a little in your programme until the cause of the problem is overcome before continuing towards your goal. The more time that is spent in getting the basics right, the less you will have to sort out later on.

Whatever you are aiming for, it is most important that this is a realistic goal for the horse concerned, also taking into account the competence and experience of the rider. So often, one or other may be quite capable but, as a combination, they are doubtful starters. An experienced rider on a young or inexperienced horse may be fine but turn the equation round the other way and it may prove disastrous.

CHOOSING THE RIGHT HORSE
Conformation

This is important as, however good a jumper it is, the cross country horse has to withstand enormous pressure and physical stress – it is essential therefore it has the conformation to cope with these.

The jumping horse must have a sound basic conformation, although it is a well-known fact that many of the world's top stars lack some of the so-called ideal attributes. Good limbs and feet, strength through the girth, an overall impression of balance and proportion, and a pleasing appearance and head are universally accepted as a good start.

The head, eye and ears can tell you a lot about the horse and its temperament. I like a horse with a forehead that is broad and flat between the eyes, not a horse with an 'obstinate' bump or one that has a particularly dished face. The eye should be large, kind and generous, not too small or piggy, which usually indicates an obstinate or ungenerous horse. I do not particularly like a horse with the white of its eye showing too much, but if it is large and bold, I can forgive this. Large ears usually denote a workmanlike horse. Small ears are nice only on a pony.

The way the head is set on to the neck and how this comes out of the shoulder can affect the whole balance of the horse and how it moves, so this is an important consideration in a dressage or jumping horse, particularly in an eventer which is expected to perform well in the dressage arena too. The neck should come out of the top of the shoulder, and should have a good length and topline curve. Horses that have an overstrong bottom line or are ewe-necked are usually strong and rubbery in the head, and thus awkward to steer and control. Those with low-set necks have more weight to support on their front end, and thus tend to be on their forehand and often ride heavy in the hand.

The withers should be well defined in order to keep the saddle in the right place. The shoulders should be strong but not heavy and should have a good slope to them, which allows the horse to move freely. Horses with straight shoulders are often rather restricted movers and can be a little stilted in their action.

This horse has good conformation and a kind, sensible expression. The back is a little on the long side but this is acceptable in mares. The limbs and feet are good and the quarters strong and muscular.

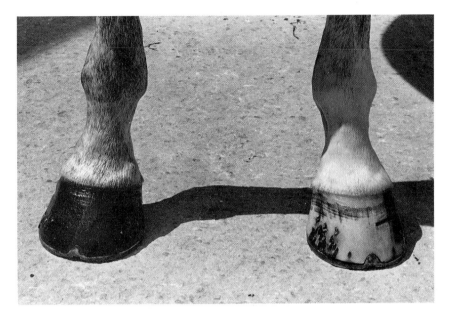

Although different colours, these feet are a good shape.

The back should be in proportion to the build and height of the horse, neither too long, which can indicate weakness, nor too short, which can prevent freedom and scope. The depth through the girth is usually a good indication of the horse's strength. If the girth is deep and the back a little long it will probably be a tough horse, and a good galloper and jumper, but the long, shallow horse is likely to be less robust.

The quarters are the power source of the horse and these should be strong and muscular. The tail should be well set on, not too low, and the overall picture should be one of strength when looked at both from the back and the side. A horse that is 'split' up the back, lacking muscle between the hind legs, is prone to weakness. A horse that clamps its tail down or holds it out to one side may well have a back problem and should be thoroughly checked over by your vet.

The hind legs should be strong through the second thigh (gaskin) and hocks. Sickle hocks are prone to weakness. An even angle from hip to stifle to hock usually gives a good indication as to the strength of the 'back end'. The pasterns should be strong and sloping, with short cannons. The joints should be flat and clean, not showing wear or puffiness, which indicates strain.

The front limbs should match those at the back and the horse should look well balanced. There should be adequate breadth between the front

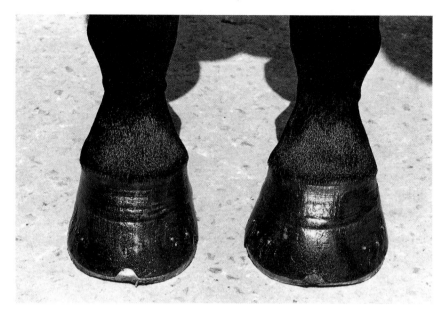

Study the feet carefully when buying a horse. These feet are not quite a pair, which could indicate a problem or simply be caused by careless shoeing.

This foot has a good heel and the angle from the fetlock through the pastern and hoof is fairly good. The toe, however, could be cut back a little more.

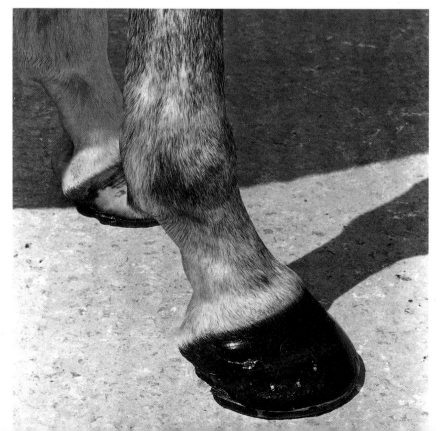

legs, matching that at the back, so that the horse has 'a leg at each corner', and there is an overall impression of balance and proportion. The knees should be strong and flat and the animal should not give the appearance of being 'back' at the knee, which could put extra strain on the tendons. Horses that are straight or very slightly 'over' at the knee are usually less likely to suffer from strains. The pasterns should be strong and gently sloping – not too upright, so that the horse is prone to jarring, nor so long and weak that strain is likely.

The feet support the full weight of the horse and are of vital consideration, bearing in mind that the eventer has to move fast in all types of going. Strength is essential. The feet should be rounded and shod at the correct angle, giving an evenly sloping line from the pastern through the foot. Beware of weak, flat feet with long, shallow heels. Upright, boxy feet are also bad as they tend to cause jarring. Extremes of either shape will prevent the foot from meeting the ground at the correct angle, causing undue strain on tendons and joints.

General Assessment

As well as showing the desired physical attributes, the character and temperament of the horse must be suitable as this is likely to be of great influence in competition work and will be the deciding factor in choosing an event horse. It might be nearly perfect in conformation but be a nervous wreck to ride, or have a wonderful temperament and be a brilliant jumper but have several defects in its make and shape. The important things to decide are whether you live with its faults and/or overcome or improve them in a horse that you otherwise feel sure is the right one for you. Never be forced into buying any animal unless you are really happy with it and at least have had a vet confirm that it is basically sound in heart, eye, wind and limb and, in his or her opinion, physically capable of doing the job you require. There are always plenty more horses to choose from but it is also easy to spend weeks looking for the perfect horse; like humans, they seldom exist!

UNDERSTANDING YOUR HORSE

Once you have bought your horse, it is vital to get to know it and thoroughly understand its way of thinking as this will be invaluable when it comes to negotiating the bigger courses, where a good partnership is so essential. Watch and learn how it reacts to different situations and whether this affects its jumping. Get to know if it is spooky, lacks self-confidence or is short of scope over wider fences or when jumping uphill, etc. With these, or any other, shortcomings it is vital to start building up confidence early on, by giving a sharp kick at the right moment or whatever else is required to make any situation easier rather than a potential confidence-breaker. You must be aware – the horse must be responsive!

When things go wrong they must be put right immediately. A good rider should be able to feel if stronger riding is required, more freedom or less, or perhaps a return to basic schooling. Some problems are caused by overconfidence, or by a lack of discipline or obedience, so that the horse takes over. Obedience is vital in the eventer if accidents are not to occur, so always ensure that the horse is performing as you would like. The horse must have a healthy respect for its rider and you must build up its confidence and obedience so that it will respond immediately to your every request. To be safe over the bigger fences, it is vital that the horse

Getting to know your horse, its expressions and moods and how it reacts to things is very important if you want to build up a true partnership, so vital with an event horse. Here, the horse on the left looks uncertain and grumpy; the horse on the right looks relaxed and interested.

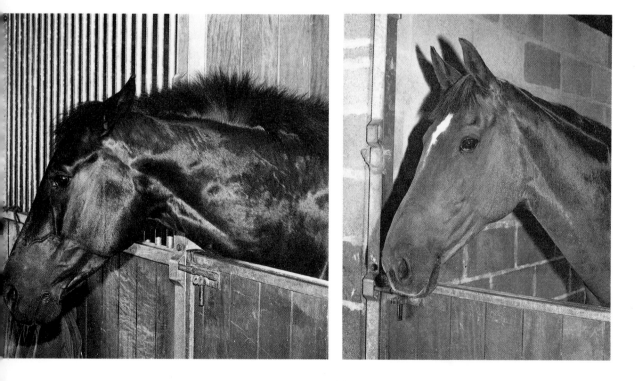

will react at once when you ask for more, or come back to you instantly when required to do so. Work on this essential obedience.

Many horses are supersensitive and could, in the right hands, be brilliant. The rider must be aware of this and may have to be prepared to adapt their style of riding quite dramatically and consistently to be able to get the best out of a particular horse. Consistency of style and technique is one of the things that helps a horse to trust its rider. It is no good hanging on to the head in front of a fence one moment and then 'dropping' the horse on to its forehand the next. Some horses simply lose confidence because of the unpredictability of such treatment.

The balance of the rider will often affect the horse's ability over a fence, so remaining in a good position throughout the approach, take-off, jump and landing is obvious but becomes particularly important with the hypersensitive type of horse.

THE YOUNG EVENTER

For those horses that have been given a proper chance, there is every hope that the rider/horse combination will reach the top. I generally like to start my horses off in their eventing careers as six-year-olds, having spent their fifth year learning the ropes of the three phases. I try to get them confident and settled in dressage classes and do quite a bit of novice show jumping so that the arenas hold no terrors for them and they know what is expected.

In the autumn of its fifth year, the horse is taken on sponsored rides, does some hunter trials and, if at all possible, goes cubbing. I am convinced that hunting teaches the horse more than any number of grids or schooling. It helps the horse to cope with uneven terrain, while standing around the coverts also teaches patience.

When cubbing, as opposed to hunting proper, there should not be too many horses to act as a distraction. Whether there are jumps or not is less important than for the horse to learn to handle itself in many different types of ground condition. Hard, soft, wet or slippery, the horse must learn to adjust to such ground, keep its feet and balance and find that 'fifth leg' when needed. Nowhere is this better learnt than going up and down steep hills or when heading towards a crowded gateway and then having to stop suddenly. This all requires a continuous change of balance, which will help the horse to become more adept at looking after itself.

It is not until their sixth year that most horses are physically mature enough to start eventing seriously. This obviously very much depends on the horse and its breeding as some are ready a bit earlier, while others may take considerably longer. Every horse will need to be assessed individually and none should be rushed. So many 'potential' stars are ruined by being asked to do too much before they are physically and mentally ready to cope.

EARLY EVENTS

The best method in all forms of training is to leave it to the horse to tell you when it is ready to progress further. After your initial schooling and practice outings, you will inevitably have taken the horse to a mini one-day event or Pre-Novice competition. Depending on how this goes and your own experience, a decision then has to be taken as to whether to stay at this level for a couple of competitions or move on to the next stage. Very often it is best to consolidate your position by remaining at the lower levels for a bit longer so that the horse sees a variety of courses at this height and learns how to cope with the various problems that are set without getting worried. It will then be easier to push on later if confidence is already established. For the horse with good, average ability, a few Pre-Novice or training events should be enough if it has had adequate schooling beforehand. Thereafter, the horse can progress to Novice or Preliminary level, where it should remain until it has thoroughly learnt the basics and knows how to cope with all eventualities in competition. A year spent at this level will pay off later as the horse will have had sufficient time to meet most variations of the different types of fence: bounces, angled rails, steps, banks, drops, corners, water jumps, etc (see Chapter 4). If all of these have been negotiated safely after eight to twelve events, now is the time to consider whether to move up to the next stage if your actual success has not already dictated this.

At Intermediate levels the horse will be expected to cope with more serious questions at up to 7.5 cm (3 in) higher than at Novice level. The horse now needs to be even more obedient to the rider and better balanced than was perhaps necessary at the lower standard. A double bounce, three steps instead of two, steeper steps up and down or a double coffin with two ditches may all be encountered. If the horse goes well over all of these, you will soon be thinking about aiming for a three-day event once you have obtained the necessary qualifications. This usually involves clear rounds at a certain number of one-day events to ensure that the horse is confident at that level before taking it to the ultimate test.

Early competitions give the horse the vital experience that is so necessary for the future. Whether it is a mini one-day event or even a team chase, as shown here, it will all go towards helping to build up the horse's confidence.

THE MENTAL APPROACH OF THE RIDER

A rider who is keen to get to the top requires a determined but adaptable mentality, with a positive attitude to everything. A competitive spirit will certainly help but this should not dominate to the extent that the welfare of the horse is ever put at risk.

As with the horse, confidence in the rider is everything, therefore a carefully structured build-up to the ultimate goal must be planned. There are, and will continue to be, numerous 'flash in the pan' riders, who sail to the top through sheer good luck, grit and determination on the day, but there are only a handful who can regularly come out and do well over a long period of time.

Knowing when to do things and when not to is one of the top riders' greatest assets. A gradual build-up, a structured programme, consistent riding, the ability to accept criticism and act on it, adaptability, a consistent but flexible style that will quickly adapt to the horse being ridden are all attributes that help the top riders to stay at the top. The will to win and a steely, inner grit and determination to succeed are what make a star. It is not always easy to keep picking up the pieces when things are going wrong but do so you must, as well as being prepared to persevere and work out why things are going wrong until the problem is solved.

Hard work and dedication have taken most of the top riders to where they are and few achieve success without a lot of graft along the way. Some have natural talent, known as 'feel' (which is always a bonus), others have to learn their craft through time and experience.

In competition, so much depends on what the aim of that particular day is to be. If it is to be used more as a schooling outing, then riding the course becomes more like an everyday workout in a competitive atmosphere, but if it is important to do well, some period of mental preparation is involved. The rider must take the time to think the day through and plan it, inform the back-up team of what needs to be done and then ride the horse in the best way to achieve those aims. Riding to win seldom just happens; it requires preparation, a mental psyching-up and then determination to see it through.

THE PHYSICAL PREPARATION OF THE RIDER

The dedicated rider is generally kept fairly fit through everyday riding, but for cross country riding it is necessary to be extremely fit in order to help your horse when it is needed yet maintain your position in the saddle and be mentally alert enough to cope with the problems that will arise along the way. Some people stay fit quite easily, while others need to work harder. Much depends on your own body metabolism and how much physical exercise you take every day, depending on your lifestyle. For those who find riding is not enough, a little extra general stable work, such as mucking out or grooming, can help considerably.

Some people prefer to go to health clubs where work in the gym on various apparatuses, including the treadmill and bicycling machine, will be particularly beneficial. Swimming, cycling, walking, jogging and dancing are all excellent. Remember that it is important to work both sides of the body evenly, so these forms of exercise are more beneficial to the rider than, say, tennis or squash which mostly use one arm. In moderation, however, all forms of sport or exercise will help considerably in improving your general level of fitness.

It must be remembered that a tired rider can considerably hinder the horse's progress round a course. When a rider is unfit, their muscles will take up most of the oxygen in the body. As these tire, so the brain becomes short of oxygen and loses its ability to concentrate and function properly. Once the rider's pulse goes above 120 beats per minute for any significant length of time, it will begin to affect their ability to concentrate and make decisions! You owe it to your horse to be in a fit state to look

The physical demands on the rider are quite strenuous, particularly at three-day events where the rider will be in the saddle, jumping numerous different fences, for some time. Rider fitness is as important as that of the horse.

after it all the way round the course! It is pointless being paranoid about your horse's fitness without taking equal care of your own.

While everyday riding will keep you in good trim for most Novice competitions, for Advanced, three-day events or serious team chasing, it is necessary to spend extra time on your own fitness build-up. Running and skipping are the two exercises I have always found I could do most easily, along with running up plenty of stairs and a bit of bicycling. All through your training, remember to think consciously about breathing in and out correctly. It is amazing how many experienced riders fail to realize that they do not breathe correctly all the time but are holding their breath in certain situations.

Cross country riding itself is very strenuous because of the ups and downs of the terrain, the different types of fence, the length of time you must hold your muscles in jumping position, etc. This may be only for five to six minutes in a one-day event or team chase, but could be from ten to thirteen minutes or so at a big three-day event, and this can seem like a very long time unless you are fit and well prepared for it. Keep your own fitness up to scratch, along with that of your horse.

THE MUSCULAR STRUCTURE OF THE HORSE

The horse has adapted remarkably well to being ridden and selective breeding over the years has ensured that the modern sports horse is basically ready in mind and body for the demands made of it. However, big fences, the often hilly terrain and the weight and balance of the rider can all contribute towards injury unless care is taken to minimize the risks. When in good health, the horse's body should be strong, with an ability to contract and relax all muscles when required.

For the jumping horse, the muscles in the hindquarters and back are by far the most important. Until these are strong enough, the horse should not be asked to do strenuous work or serious jumping. Once the horse has reached maturity, the introduction of training exercises, to build up strength and balance, will, in time, help to produce the maximum performance of which that horse is capable. The best way of building up muscles is through work and it is best to start your fitness work on the flat, to loosen, make supple and build up the horse's ability and strength thoroughly. Once basic fitness has been established, hillwork, if possible, and then more serious training, again on the flat, can start.

The back, shoulder and quarter muscles are those most affected in the jumping horse. How the horse moves, its straightness of action and its general conformation will all affect its ultimate jumping ability. Various people prefer different conformation attributes but so long as the horse is of a reasonable make and shape, has strong limbs capable of supporting its body, moves straight and is well prepared for the job, it is character and temperament, in conjunction with proper training and riding, that will turn it into a superstar, rather than whether it is the ideal shape.

In eventing the risk of injury is high because of the very nature of the sport, so early training and a strict, gradual build-up to peak fitness, before asking too much of the horse, cannot be overemphasized. It is most important that the rider trains the horse in such a way that the right muscles are developed to help to attain their ultimate goals. Training should encourage the horse to be loose and supple but strong, and this is achieved by the horse and rider working in harmony as a partnership while confidence and muscle strength increase.

The horse is remarkably adaptable to being ridden by humans. Occasionally, however, tendons or a muscle in the shoulder, back or quarters can be pulled or put under strain. This can be due to a variety of causes, ranging from uneven feet or badly fitting tack to falls and poor riding techniques.

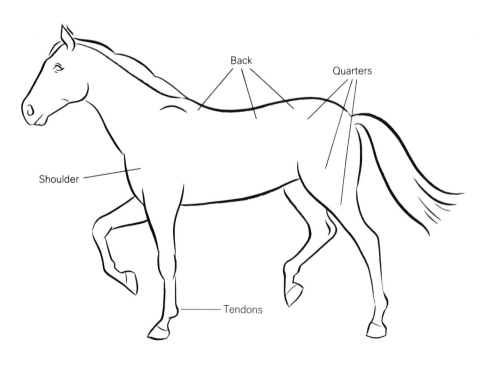

The horse's reflexes play a most important role in how well muscles react and respond. This reaction to a stimulus is very important as it is the rider's means of communication but the rider must be quick to note the horse's reactions and respond accordingly. So often, at the lower levels, horses are seen being kicked along incessantly but showing little reaction because their reflex to this has become deadened by the same, continuous stimulus. The rider must feel whether the horse is receptive or not and, through careful schooling, build on this so that, the moment a reaction is felt, the stimulus ceases until it is required again.

Many of the horse's reflexes are involuntary, such as those used when the horse moves or jumps and those which affect balance. The horse uses its head and neck as its main means of balance. How it does this can make a big difference in its ability to jump well and the rider should understand the basic principles behind the way in which the horse jumps.

How the horse jumps.

How the Horse Jumps

As it approaches a fence, the horse raises its head, the hind legs bend a little more and the forelegs stretch out before coming up off the ground. At the same time, the horse's hind legs come forward, push down, then stretch into the leap up and over the fence. The strength of this leap determines how high or wide the horse will jump over the fence. In the air, the horse should have the freedom to stretch and lower its head, keeping its back well arched over the fence. As the horse descends, the front legs separate so that one foreleg touches the ground first, taking all the horse's weight for a split second before the other foreleg touches down. The hind legs then come down together as the first foreleg comes up off the ground to take the first stride away from the fence. This first stride tends to be rather long and flat, and it is vital that the rider stays in balance, being neither behind nor in front of the movement at this critical stage.

Throughout the jump, various reflexes will take over to allow muscles to contract and extend during the different parts of the jump. The position of the rider and their ability to 'go with the horse' over each fence will influence every jump. A rider who throws his or her body forward during a jump will immediately tip the horse's balance forward and push it on to its forehand, forcing it down in front, as will the rider who gets too far forward on take off. When this occurs, the horse is likely to hit the fence in front.

Riders who sit up too quickly once the horse has taken off, or who get left behind, will restrict the forward momentum. They usually end up with their seat in the saddle and then catch the horse in the mouth, causing an immediate tightening of the back muscles and a raising of the head, with the result that the hind legs contract instead of reaching their full extension, and the horse hits the fence, usually with its hind legs.

This rider is learning to jump fences at an angle. Note that her knee has come away from the saddle, which weakens her security. Here, a practice ditch has been made out of sacks and poles.

At combination fences, where the horse has to make quick adjustments in balance in order to jump two or more fences in quick succession, the reflexes and muscles must react very quickly but the well-trained horse should cope well as long as the rider remains still and balanced throughout. A rider who keeps interfering makes such adjustments very difficult for the horse. The short-striding horse is, however, likely to find such fences easier than an onward-going, long-striding horse.

THE HORSE'S TEMPERAMENT

The temperament of the horse will greatly affect its way of going, training and general improvement, but the rider's understanding of the horse and the way he or she adapts to and copes with it will determine how successful the partnership becomes. Some people can get on any horse and, through 'feel', adapt to that horse and get a good tune out of it straightaway, while others thoroughly upset the horse because they force when they should coax, niggle when they should sit quietly, do not encourage when they should or just simply cannot, or will not, adapt to the horse's way of going, asking it, instead, to change its natural way of going to suit them, whether it is well schooled or not. The good rider should be able to adapt to the horse and then get the best out of it through sympathetic riding and correct schooling. Riders who impose their will forcefully on a horse are rarely successful, although some horses *do* require strong riding and a fairly positive approach to bring out the best in them.

The cross country horse must be bold. It must be the sort of horse that takes its fences on once it has been properly trained and schooled, even if it was a bit timid beforehand. There is nothing worse than riding a horse that does not go forwards over big, solid timber. The worst mistake a rider can make is to overrestrict a horse going round a cross country course. By doing this, each fence becomes an effort because of the lack of impulsion and the horse will soon lose confidence unless the rider accepts the problem and changes their way of riding. It is vital to acknowledge one's faults and mistakes if progress is to be made, so always work out why problems arise, and then act on this.

It is important to assess each horse individually and discover what makes it 'tick'. Some require very sympathetic, quiet riding, others need pushing into every fence, some require careful balancing before a fence, others are best left entirely alone to sort themselves out. Nowadays, the use of video cameras has made it possible to study horses in action, which can be very revealing and helpful, especially when contemplating the purchase of a horse or for use during schooling.

Assessing how to ride it and what really works with your particular horse can be quite a challenging occupation. Its speed, bitting, degree of training and technique over a fence can all affect the end result, so think it all through and try different methods, bits or whatever until you feel confident that you have the best combination for that horse.

Remember that the potential eventer or cross country horse needs to be a good all rounder, not necessarily just a sensational jumper. Its technique or ability should show promise, and it needs to be quick thinking and able to learn from its mistakes. When trying a horse, I am always pleased if it makes a mistake so that I can watch how it reacts next time. If it really tries next time, you can be satisfied that it has a brain – if it makes the same mistake again, you need to think about your life insurance! This, of course, does not necessarily follow with a real youngster.

This horse looks a little anxious as it takes off over a log with a drop landing but, with firm coaxing from its rider, it looks quite confident again a split second later.

THE PACES OF THE HORSE

For the cross country horse the most important pace is canter, and you must also assess whether the horse can increase and decrease the canter stride. If it can do this well, it is likely to be able to gallop adequately. It is always said that a horse with a good walk also gallops well. If it has a good shoulder, with plenty of freedom in it, it should be able to gallop. A horse with a very upright shoulder may be rather restricted and have a short, choppy stride. Correct schooling can help but, if the conformation is poor, the horse is unlikely to be able to achieve the same reach and length of stride of a horse that has a good sloping shoulder.

The most important thing to consider in all paces is whether the horse is going forward and whether it is straight. Any one-sidedness will affect how you approach and jump fences, so work on this from day one. One of the most basic essentials that is often neglected as a really important part of the horse's early training is that going forward and straight are two vital points for the cross country horse.

When coming towards such imposing fences as the Vicarage Vee at Badminton there really is no room for error – there is a stretch of approximately only 61 cm (2 ft) that is safe for most horses to jump before you either miss the fence altogether or put yourself in the situation of taking dangerous risks by going too far to the other side of the fence where it is hopelessly wide. Other fences, such as corners or angled rails, also require a straight approach. Nothing is more frightening than approaching a fence on a horse that is not going where you want it to go when you are in a strong gallop. The horse must be obedient to the rider's wishes and respond evenly on either side.

For cross country work, the horse needs to stay in an even rhythm throughout, taking free, balanced strides. It is important that the horse does not lose that rhythm. There is nothing worse than watching a horse being pulled out of any rhythm it might have had.

When galloping, again rhythm is the most important aspect, together with the ability of the rider to maintain their balance towards, over and away from the fences. If the initial flat work has been conscientiously carried out, it should be possible to shorten or lengthen the stride as necessary without in any way altering the rhythm. By closing the legs and lifting the hands a little, any alteration in pace or balance should be easily achieved on a well-trained horse.

In all paces the rider must practise shortening and lengthening the stride so that the horse becomes obedient and responsive. The horse must remain in balance and not begin to hurry as it is asked to lengthen

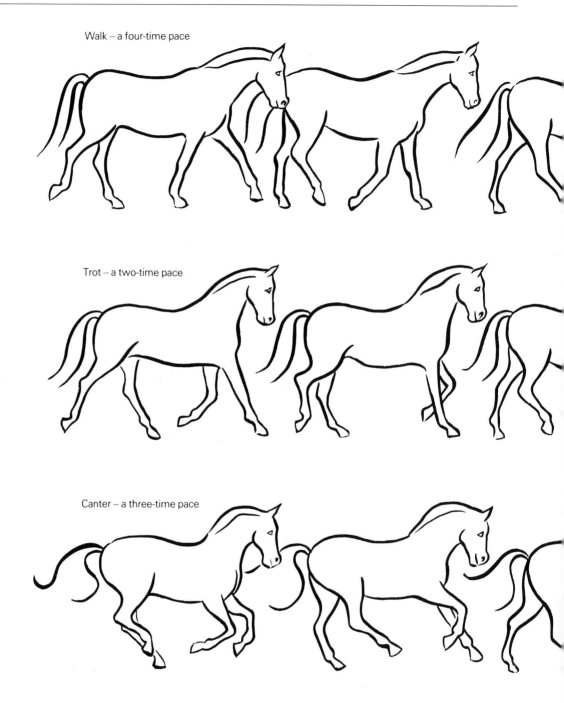

Walk – a four-time pace

Trot – a two-time pace

Canter – a three-time pace

It is worth spending time in developing the horse's paces so that it can shorten and lengthen in each when required. For the jumping phases the canter becomes the most important pace, so spend plenty of time on this in your early schooling.

but to stretch forward instead and take a longer stride – not a quicker one. Transitions from one pace to another, or within that pace, must be loose and supple and not restricted – you must never lose the forward movement but should create greater impulsion with your legs and seat. Work at each pace will be more closely examined later (see p.58), but always keep it in the back of your mind that you can improve your horse's way of going by being quite strict with yourself and the horse as much when out hacking as when schooling. Of course, the young horse, in particular, must be allowed to relax when out hacking but it must also pay attention when asked. Do not nag on at the horse but keep its attention by asking different questions and always make sure you get the response you want when you want it, not at any old time.

By ensuring that your horse responds at all times when asked, you are less likely to have problems in gallop on a cross country course – it cannot be overstressed that obedience is everything and will affect how each phase of the competition is carried out. How much time you spend on this depends on the horse's fitness, but obedience starts in the stable, on the lunge and out in the field as much as when the horse is ridden, and it must learn to respect and respond to its rider at all times.

2

STABLE MANAGEMENT

It is assumed that the readers of this book are thoroughly competent horsemasters and the following points are discussed only as being specifically relevant to the better preparation of the cross country horse.

I am a great believer in producing the horse to be a tough contender in the rugged sports of eventing and team chasing. In my opinion, therefore, the horse should not be treated in the same way as a show horse, where, for example, the coat and general condition and appearance of the horse play such a major part. The eventer has to compete in all weathers and in all going, so it must be prepared for these conditions too. Uncomfortable as it might be, the horse will have to practise a dressage test in the rain and must learn to put up with this and with the wind blowing at the same time. Within reason, the horse must continue to concentrate and must perform under all conditions as the event is unlikely to be halted every time there is a shower and some of these can be very heavy!

For this reason, therefore, you should exercise in all weathers, so that, on the day, this will not present anything unusual for the horse – just unpleasant. For this reason, I rarely use a paddock sheet when exercising in cold or bad weather, unless the horse is clipped out and is only at the walking stage of its training. You can work it quite hard to keep it warm, even when walking, by the degree of collection you ask for or by doing a little shoulder-in, half-halts, extending the pace or whatever. Keep the horse moving fairly briskly but do not overcosset it and then expect it to be tough on the day if you have always protected it from the elements. When starting horses in work I generally give them a blanket or racing clip until they are working enough to make them sweat. They are clipped out before their coats start to change.

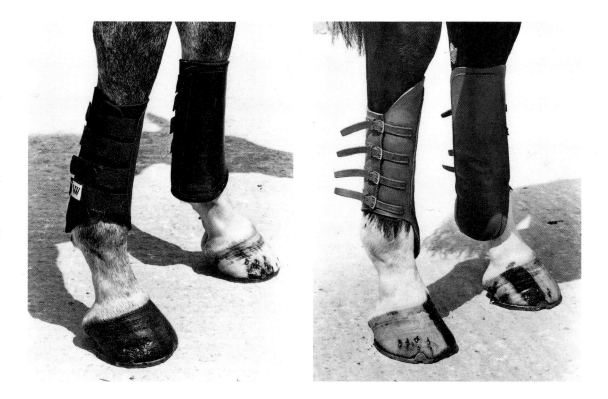

Two types of leg protection, which will help to prevent everyday bumps and bruises. If Velcro fastenings are used for cross country work, they should be taped for extra security, especially if it is wet or muddy or there is water to negotiate.

BOOTS

Boots to protect the legs are, in most cases, a sensible precaution but, occasionally, you will find that some horses tend to be rubbed by these. If your horse goes very close behind or in front then you will obviously need protection and you will have to experiment to find out what suits your horse best. If, however, it goes quite wide, you may be better off without boots except when schooling or lungeing. Some horses are only close behind, so probably only require hind boots; others will require only fronts.

Whatever you use, it is absolutely vital that you feel the legs carefully every day to ensure there are no sores or scabs which could harbour infection as these could quickly work up the leg and put your horse out of action.

I am a great believer in washing the legs off thoroughly with pure soap after galloping, following a competition or if I have been through sticky mud, as I believe this is the best way of removing the combination of sweat and dirt that accumulates under a boot and can cause irritation. Be very careful with detergents of any sort or use only the very mildest type on your horse in case it reacts to this. After washing off the legs, dry them thoroughly. Some horses tend to develop rather dry, chapped legs if this is done too often as there is always a danger that you are removing natural oils from the skin, so avoid doing this more than once or twice a week, especially with horses that have white legs.

Following a workout or competition, I usually put dry bandages on overnight. If the ground has been hard and jarring, I might use kaolin or a commercial cooling lotion instead. The bandages are removed early the next morning and the legs left to cool for an hour or two before being checked thoroughly and a decision made as to whether the horse will be ridden, led out or turned out, depending very much on its temperament and likely behaviour. On fit horses, that do not always go out every day, protective boots are used if they are likely to gallop about.

It is essential that all boots or bandages are kept scrupulously clean. They should either be dried thoroughly and then brushed with a stiff brush or washed carefully. Remember not to use strong detergents in case the horse reacts to these, or at least be sure to rinse them thoroughly after washing.

SHOEING

The importance of correct shoeing cannot be overemphasized and it really is up to the owner or rider to learn the basic requirements of good shoeing to ensure that they give their horse the best possible chance of staying sound. Regular footcare is essential and it is no good leaving the horse for an extra week just because its shoes are not worn or the clenches have not come up. Growth always takes place and once the angle of the foot becomes out of line, distortion of the foot will quickly occur. Many vets believe that a very high percentage of lameness is foot-related. It is vital to discuss your horse's feet with your farrier, look carefully to see that the angle and balance of the foot are correct and arrange for visits on a regular basis. Ask him to point out your horse's good and bad points, to explain what you should be looking out for and, if necessary, how, between you, it might be possible to improve the foot itself over a period of time.

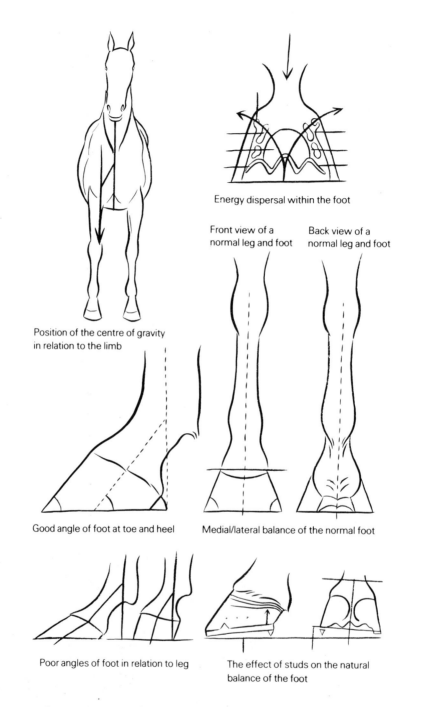

Energy dispersal within the foot

Front view of a normal leg and foot

Back view of a normal leg and foot

Position of the centre of gravity in relation to the limb

Good angle of foot at toe and heel

Medial/lateral balance of the normal foot

Poor angles of foot in relation to leg

The effect of studs on the natural balance of the foot

Correct shoeing is extremely important. These diagrams show good and poor hoof angles and the detrimental effect on the foot of using studs, especially big ones, on hard ground, when the weight is distributed down the legs to the feet with increased force to the inside and the front.

The farrier cannot put things right all in one go if the feet have been neglected. It may take several months gradually to change the angle of the foot if things are bad. There are many different shoes that can be used, either to spread the weight over a wider area or give extra support to the foot or parts of it. If fairly dramatic changes are required, these are best done during a quiet period so that the horse can adjust to the change without strain.

STUDS

The use of studs is always a difficult decision as, although they help considerably in preventing the horse from slipping and sliding, they also interfere with the angle of the foot every time they are used. In Britain, riders tend to use just one stud in each shoe, on the outside. In America and the rest of Europe, riders usually use two, one on either side.

Most farriers will tell you that they are opposed to the use of studs in principle, however there is no doubt that, in certain ground conditions, they help considerably to minimize the risk of slipping. Over the years I have tried using different studs in different ground conditions, starting

The use of studs can help considerably in slippery conditions but think carefully how they will affect the horse when choosing which ones to use.

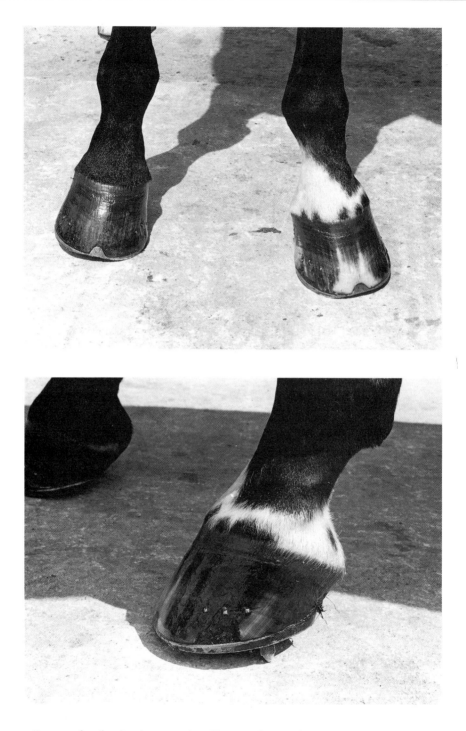

On very hard going large studs will not sink into the ground and may jar the horse instead. These two photographs show the tilting effect that occurs on hard surfaces when one stud only is used.

To save time on the day of the competition, it is recommended that stud holes are cleaned out the previous day and filled with oiled cotton wool or blank studs.

with the very big ones, but I have now refined my ideas to the following criteria: in good ground conditions, no studs at all; in wet, greasy conditions, large studs behind (medium ones in front for more unbalanced horses only); on slightly slippery ground, as when the grass is still wet from dew etc., medium ones behind, road studs (small) in front; on hard ground I use the smallest I can find (in front or all around, to suit the horse), which just break up the top surface.

My feeling is that studs are necessary for most horses, except for those that are really well balanced and who can probably cope quite easily without them. In greasy or hard conditions, studs are probably required by almost all horses.

It is in hard ground conditions that studs are likely to do the most damage to the horse because of the jarring effect of the ground and the fact that using them has tilted the angle of the foot so, with the ground being hard, this will not sink into the ground so easily. At the end of the day, however, you have to weigh up the pros and cons and make your own decisions. Think about the length of time you intend to leave the studs in the shoe. If your horse has had a long day and has had to stand on the rigid floor of a lorry for a long time, it is unlikely that supporting its weight at an unaccustomed angle for any length of time will do it any good. Take the studs out or stand the horse outside if it is quiet but do be aware of the effect your studs could be having on its feet, especially the front ones if it has rather sensitive feet or suspect legs.

CARE OF THE FEET

Make sure you pay attention to your horse's feet and continually check them to ensure they remain in good shape and condition. Oil and dress them as necessary, especially if they become dry and brittle in hot weather. Watch out for thrush, which is prone to developing in damp weather or if the bedding is always wet. Such a condition can appear very quickly. Ask your farrier to trim carefully round the frog where thrush can become prevalent. Spray regularly with an antibiotic spray if necessary.

LEG CARE

You must become very familiar with your horse's legs if you are going to be able to detect the first sign of a problem. Always treat any heat or swelling with suspicion and make quite sure that it is completely cured before putting the horse back into full work again. Any tendon problem is always serious but superficial bruising can also initially present like a strain. Cold hosing is always of benefit with bruising or in the early stages of a strain, so if you have any worries, hose the suspect site and keep it cold until your vet can examine it properly.

Generally, I do not bandage my horses in the stable except on the night following a competition or serious gallop. In this way, I believe one can observe any changes to the legs more easily and also you do not soften the legs so much. I tend to believe that the horse will feel a knock far more if it has been cosseted under bandages and so will swell up more than if it is better accustomed to little everyday bumps and bruises. Some horses, however, do seem to blow up at the slightest thing, while others do not. I think colour makes a slight difference. Strong bays and dark browns generally appear to be slightly tougher than chestnuts or greys. White legs or certainly those with pink, rather than dark, skin appear slightly more prone to skin infections and rubs or sores.

I try to make a point of feeling the horse's legs every evening and always before tacking up if I have not already seen them. If you feel them

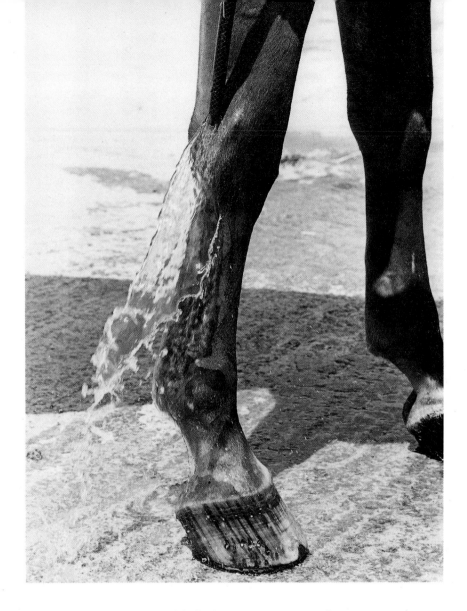

*Cold hosing is invaluable for bruises or any signs of strain. A gentle,
continuous stream is required. If you have one nearby, standing in a clean,
running stream is another way of achieving the same benefit.*

morning and evening and keep a true image of how they feel in your
mind, asking yourself in particular whether they are a pair, you are likely
to pick up the early signs of problems. If you can spot these before they
start, you will have few worries.

The weather, what they are fed and the amount of work they do can
and will affect the state of horses' legs. In hot weather the legs inevitably
fill a bit; in cold they always feel better. Too much food often causes the
legs to swell and more harm is done by overfeeding than underfeeding.

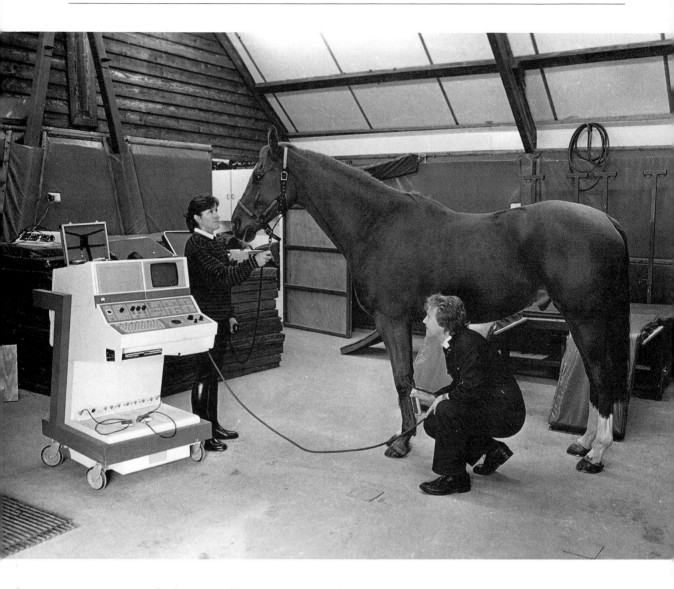

Early detection of leg problems is vital. A leg scan can determine the extent of any damage and scans are now regularly used to diagnose tendon injuries.

FEEDING

Feeding is an art in itself and something that takes years of experience to perfect. However, with so much information now available, it should be possible for everyone to gain enough knowledge at least to work on. The biggest mistake that tends to be made is that of giving too much protein in the diet. The competition horse requires plenty of digestible energy and does not need a huge concentration of protein. Oats are always the feed of choice and should be fed lightly bruised or rolled. Many people feel that horses tend to 'hot up' on oats but in my experience this is not so and the fitter the horse becomes the more settled it will become. Warmbloods and other non-Thoroughbreds do sometimes become more excitable on oats, however, and may be better on barley. Barley is more fattening than oats and can be fed either rolled or micronized or as a boiled feed, when it is often mixed with linseed.

Maize is also a fattening food but is very indigestible and is not normally fed to competition horses. Beans are not recommended for the same reason, although they are very high in protein. Both these foods are to be found in the various commercially produced coarse mixes and care should be taken when choosing your mix to ensure that your horse is not receiving too much of these foods.

Compound nuts come in numerous different varieties, containing all sorts of foods, such as oats, barley, bran, maize, grass meal, molasses and various essential minerals, etc., but do ensure that you do not go for those with too high a protein content. The maximum protein content my horses have is 12 per cent, even when doing something like Badminton. Competition horses need energy foods, not the high protein ones that are necessary for growing youngsters. It is carbohydrates that provide the competition horse with most of its energy, either as cereal or roughage. Oats, barley, sugar beet and fat are all important energy sources.

Everyone has their own feeding routine and their particular likes or dislikes, based on personal experiences, but if your horse looks and feels good, seems well in itself and is coping with its work easily, it is probably eating the right diet. By looking at it objectively, check regularly to make sure its coat is loose and supple, that it is neither too fat nor too thin for its stage of fitness and that it is receiving the right sort of food for what it is expected to do, all the while remembering that each horse is an individual.

Some people make the mistake of feeding extras, such as a variety of minerals and supplements, plus endless herbs and potions. Most mixes and compound foods have balanced ingredients, with the correct amount of vital minerals and vitamins added. By adding extras, the feed ratios become completely unbalanced and, in some cases, have caused poisoning. If a supplement or vitamin is necessary, select one that provides what is required and then stick to that. Do not make your horse ill by overloading it with unnecessary additives – the only person who then benefits is the salesman who sells it to you.

Of course, some horses do have slight problems of dietary deficiency and such horses should certainly be given any necessary supplements *after* consultation with your vet but, otherwise, let the horse benefit from a naturally balanced diet, uncluttered with endless so-called 'essentials'.

There are numerous different types of food on the market. The event horse requires a high-energy diet suitable for the work it is doing. Do not feed too much protein when the horse is in light work.

WORMING, VACCINATION AND TEETH CARE

Month	Worming	Teeth	Flu/vacs/etc
January		Rasp	Vaccinate
March	Broad Spectrum		
May			
July	Broad Spectrum	Check	Check
September			
November	Broad Spectrum		

Keeping a simple chart, such as this, can act as a reminder to ensure that a regular worming programme is carried out. Remember to check when flu vaccinations are due and to have the horse's teeth rasped at least once a year. A broad spectrum wormer is effective against most worms. It is important to vary the wormers used, however, as worms can develop a resistance to the wormers if you use the same one all the time.

TOOTHCARE

It goes without saying that regular teeth checks are necessary to ensure there are no sharp hooks developing or that roughness anywhere is causing the horse discomfort, either in eating or from the bit. Generally, horses need their teeth rasping at least once a year, while some need this done twice yearly. Specialist horse dentists are probably more adept at rasping teeth, due to the huge numbers they do, rather than your vet who is usually delighted to pass this back-breaking chore on to another.

WORMING

The importance of a regular worming routine cannot be overemphasized, but do remember to vary the brands used according to the different times of the year and remember that not all brands dispose of every type of worm. Check your worming routine with your vet. If you have only a small turnout paddock, it is well worth picking up the droppings daily to help to keep the worm infestation down. If possible, rest the paddock for at least three months a year. A few sheep borrowed from a neighbouring farmer will do wonders for the paddock during part of this time.

If your horse does not thrive despite plenty of good food and regular worming, get a worm count done to ensure there was no build-up of worms in its system before you bought it. I always give a double dose, two weeks apart, to any new horses arriving in my yard, just in case they have not had regular worming.

CLIPPING AND RUGGING

Whether you clip your horse fully or not over the winter very much depends on the horse, how much it sweats and the amount of work it is doing. I do think it is important, however, to keep the clipped horse sufficiently warm in the winter months. If the coat becomes dry, feed some extra cod liver oil, which will help the coat and will also keep the horse warm. Much energy is lost in trying to keep warm in cold weather so it makes sense to help in this way, particularly if the horse is on the lean side.

When starting slow work, I prefer to give only a blanket or high version of a trace clip, so that the long back muscles are kept a little warmer when doing long, slow work in walk during what is usually a rather cold period after the British Christmas. I then clip them out fully before the summer coat starts to come through or leave them so that they get a good summer coat coming through anyway. This usually depends on the weather, the horse's coat and what it is doing.

Once the horse is clipped, never allow it to stand in a draught. It is surprising how easy it is to become complacent and think things like that are not important, however a little draught can send the long muscles of the back into spasm, which can be very painful if they really tighten. Tight muscles are not so readily able to work, so this horse is likely to be more difficult in training. Warmth is everything, particularly to the fit horse expected to produce its best.

FRESH AIR

Depending on the type of stabling you have, it is sometimes quite difficult to keep a continuous free flow of fresh air through your stables, which I believe to be very important to your horse's overall health. Most of the respiratory problems of today are aggravated by a lack of clean air, so try to ensure that your horse is given the best chance of receiving this, especially if it is kept in a 'barn' or in low stabling where the air is

This barn provides excellent ventilation through vents in the roof and sliding doors at either end. There is a good wide passageway between the two lines of boxes. Fresh air and good ventilation are vital if horses are to remain healthy.

unlikely to be good. Shutting top doors will often remove all chance of a flow of fresh air, so it is usually much better to put on an extra rug and keep the door open, except when the very worst weather is blowing into the stable itself. Hot, stale and stuffy air is the worst possible environment for the horse.

THE HORSE'S MENTAL HEALTH

So much time and effort is spent on the horse's physical well-being that one tends to forget the less-obvious mental side, which can be most important with some horses, especially the more sensitive ones. Stress and excitement show up in such horses in very different ways and may present in the better known stable vices of weaving, box-walking, cribbing, wind sucking and, in some cases, chewing or grabbing at things. They can also show as a lack of energy, the inability to put on weight, losing weight, head banging and other behavioural problems. Each horse needs to be carefully assessed to see what it is that worries it and how best to put this right, if possible.

It is generally accepted that a few hours, at least, out in the field every day is the ideal way of keeping the stabled horse content but this is not always practical or possible. Leading out in hand to graze may be the next best solution. This is relaxing and relieves the monotony of being confined to the stable for long periods.

Very often horses will be more settled in a different stable. Those further away from the tack or feed rooms may be quieter. Some horses dislike having horses on either side of them, particularly mares when in season. Some prefer something to look at, while others are best kept out of the way, 'round the back', if such a box exists. Location can make a big difference with the more excitable type of horse.

For the one-horse owner with a horse that pines for company, you might need to find a friend for your horse, such as a donkey or sheep, which can get rather expensive. Try everything else first but do remember that the horse is a herd animal and does not like to be alone. Some people are rather more excitable than others, which can affect the behaviour of the horses they look after. Some people can do things to or with horses that others just do not seem able to do. Many horses will be easy to catch for some people and difficult with others. It is usually a matter of confidence and trust, which seems to show up more in some people than in others. The quieter, calmer person usually has a row of relaxed, contented horses, whereas the quick, nervous type of person can sometimes transmit this to their horses.

If you have a really sensitive horse and you know that certain people make it a bit more uptight, then it is as well to keep them apart initially or at competitions. In most cases, such horses settle down with time as they get older, wiser and more relaxed.

CHOOSING TACK
Control and Bitting

Nothing is more frightening or dangerous than being out of control, so proper bitting is most important, particularly when riding across country. There are numerous bits on the market from which to choose, among them a variety of snaffles, with double joints or rollers and plastic, vulcanite, rubber or metal mouthpieces. The gag varieties seem to become more plentiful year by year, with the rings getting bigger or more numerous and the mouthpieces being produced in every possible combination.

Curb bits, in the form of pelhams and Kimblewicks, seem to be quite popular as they enable the rider to have more control with one rein. The double bridle is not often used because of the necessity to use two reins, although it is excellent with some horses if the rider is skilled at using hands and fingers independently.

The choice of bit is a very personal subject and the action can be assisted by the use of a martingale and one of the variety of nosebands available.

The Grakle is a very popular noseband for a horse that tends to cross its jaw or open its mouth excessively and it increases control with almost any bit. Very often this is all that is required to give the extra control needed. All too often, stronger bits are used when they are quite unnecessary but it is important to feel secure, so experiment when schooling or galloping, always remembering that it is the hands at the other end of the reins that affect the horse's way of going most significantly.

When choosing an alternative bit, think carefully about *how* the horse is pulling. Does it seem that the bit is uncomfortable or is the horse leaning on the hand because it is not being ridden with enough leg? Is it frightened of discomfort in its mouth and merely running away from the pain? Occasionally things will improve greatly if you use a *milder* bit.

Sometimes it is simply that the sheer power of the horse takes over when it is fit and galloping and this is when careful thought must be applied to decide on the right bit to contain this energy in a manageable form. A Cornish snaffle (Scorrier), with its double rings, is quite useful as it is held in the mouth by the cheekpieces in a rather different way to other bits, so pressure is applied to a different part of the mouth.

A straight mouthpiece, rather than a jointed one, or the Dr Bristol or milder French link, with their double joints, can all change the area of pressure on the mouth. Bits with rollers, such as the magenis, copper roller, cherry roller, Waterford, etc., all supposedly prevent the horse from taking too strong a hold.

If turning or steering is the problem, a bit with cheeks should help considerably, or one with 'D' rings. A running martingale will also help the horse to turn, by keeping its head within the angle of control. If a gag is used, it is essential to remember the importance of the take and release principle, otherwise the horse will receive a constant and simultaneous downward pull on the poll together with an upwards pull in the mouth. Take a pull, then release, then take another, but keep releasing so that

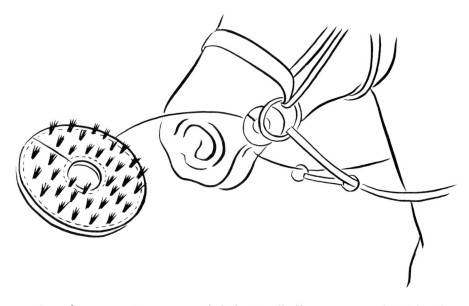

Some horses remain very one-sided, despite all efforts to correct this. A brush or pricking pad can be used to good effect when worn on the side to which the horse is unresponsive when jumping. (It cannot be worn for dressage.) First, however, you must make sure you have eliminated all other possible causes, such as sharp teeth etc.

you get a reaction each time. The bigger the rings of the gag, the more reaction you are likely to get. Keep your hands as quiet and soft as you can.

With a very one-sided horse, a 'brush' can be used to prevent it from hanging to one side and so keep it straight. You should always ask yourself why the horse is difficult to turn, in case an underlying cause can be remedied. Very often sharp teeth are the problem and then a good session with your equine dentist will work wonders. The cause may also be something more serious, such as the early symptoms of leg trouble. The horse may have developed this action as a form of compensation to reduce pain elsewhere. Investigate the legs and feet thoroughly, especially if this is a recent problem.

Whatever the trouble appears to be, do not ignore it but endeavour to get to the bottom of it as soon as possible. Try out as many different bits as possible at home and when schooling so that you know what works for you and what does not. Control is essential to success and it is worth spending a bit of time on this before setting off to an event, only to discover, too late, that you cannot stop or turn.

The Hackamore

Sometimes a complete rest from a bit is helpful. Riding in a hackamore is then the only alternative but, before venturing out into the wide, open spaces in one, spend a few days in a school or arena first, making quite sure you have adequate control as I cannot overstress the importance of acting responsibly if riding out in a hackamore. If there are any sores or bruises in the horse's mouth, spending time without a bit will give these a chance to heal properly and the horse will also have the chance to forget any worries about its mouth.

A Hackamore can be a very useful alternative if the horse has bitting problems or an injured mouth. Make sure you try it out in a confined area first, to ensure that you are in control!

If your horse is difficult in its mouth, a hackamore may prove very useful in a retraining programme. I have had considerable success in this way with two very difficult horses whose mouth problems totally defeated my repertoire of solutions. When I removed the bit completely, the horses relaxed and started to jump in a much more correct outline, moving straighter and approaching the fences more calmly. One horse remained obedient and calm in the hackamore even when outside of an enclosed environment. Although I must admit I did not feel particularly safe, it certainly jumped much better!

If you have a difficult horse, you must make the decision whether to get rid of it or to persevere. This often depends on such factors as time, your degree of patience and the money you can afford to spend. I have never found a superstar that has not been difficult at some stage during its progress to the top.

The Use of Gadgets

Nowadays there are numerous schooling aids on the market, all claiming to be the latest key to success. However, anyone who has lived and worked with horses knows that this is unlikely. There is no substitute for correct schooling and to produce a horse that is properly schooled for the job it is expected to do takes time, patience and money.

In general, gadgets do have a purpose in the right hands and can be used to great effect by those who understand what should, or should not, be expected of the horse at its stage of development and training. The running rein has been used with success for centuries. There are numerous different forms of this on the market and, as long as the basic principle of riding the horse forward into an unrestricted outline is remembered, rather than pulling the horse's head in, then this is a most helpful gadget.

Any item that restricts the horse's natural forward movement by the use of force has to be suspect in my opinion. There are some which give the horse no freedom or ability to stretch out and relax and I cannot believe this is right. Anything that is fixed has to be restricting to the horse and is not something I would use.

There are numerous gadgets for schooling horses but great care must be taken with their use to ensure that they do not do more harm than good. Running reins should never be used to pull the horse's head in, only to prevent the head from coming up too high.

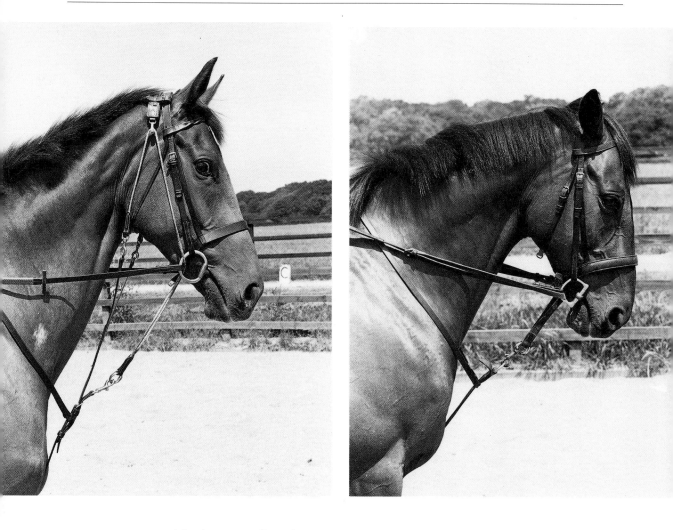

LEFT *The de Gogue allows freedom but encourages the horse to lower and stretch its head and neck, which is essential for all basic schooling. It can be fitted in two different ways, for either lungeing or riding.*

RIGHT *The Market Harborough helps to keep the head in the correct position and, when correctly fitted, only acts as a running rein if the head comes up too high. The lower part slackens as the head lowers.*

Classical aids, such as lungeing in a chambon or riding in a de Gogue, have stood the test of time. Both of these allow the horse to stretch, raise or lower its head while also encouraging a lower and rounder outline, but they never restrict the forward movement, which is the essential element in all horse training.

Of course, there are many instances where horses have been wrongly trained or rushed in training so that the end result is a nice horse with lots of talent, which has almost been ruined because its training has turned into a near horror story. It will usually take years to get such horses going as we would all like but time and money seldom allow for a proper retraining. The result is that they have to improve rapidly and never get the chance to 'unlearn' bad habits before learning new ones properly. Inevitably, gadgets are resorted to and, in some cases, do a great deal of harm. In the right, sympathetic hands, however, they can be a useful training or reschooling aid and are enormously helpful in guiding the horse in the right direction.

DEVELOPING FITNESS

Preparation and careful planning are vital if you really want to succeed. How you set about working out your programme very much depends on the standard of your horse and your ultimate aims. At the beginning of every season, it is worth spending an hour or two looking at all the options and deciding where to go with each horse, while also having an alternative schedule in case things do not go quite according to plan.

As the horse becomes more advanced, it is likely that you will only want to do sufficient events to keep its eye in, keep its qualifications up and sharpen it up in condition ready for 'the big one'. Once all the basic work has been done and the horse has learnt how to cope with the many different types of fence, there is little point in putting more miles on the clock just for the sake of it. The older, more experienced horse needs sustaining for the future, not hammering endlessly round too many courses.

PLANNING YOUR PROGRAMME

You must give careful thought as to the best programme for each horse. Some benefit from more competitions early on while others may be best with just one or two runs before a three-day event. At some stage, they should ideally jump round a course of the same standard as the fences they are going to meet in the event.

When planning your programme, decide on the event you want to ride at, then work out the fitness aspect. In general, for a Novice (★) one-star, three-day event I would allow 12 to 14 weeks to get the horse fit; 14 to 16 weeks for a (★★) two-star; 16 to 18 weeks for a (★★★) three-star and 18 to 20 weeks for a (★★★★) four-star event. This is only a rough guideline as some horses get fitter more quickly than others, depending on how long they have been off work or whether they have, in fact, been kept just ticking along.

It is a fact that getting horses really fit for the first time seems to take much longer than with those that have been well prepared and fittened before, but I still cannot overemphasize the importance of early slow work to harden and strengthen tendons, muscles and ligaments. If this part is treated really seriously, you can rest assured that at least you have given your horse the best start in its preparations. Thereafter, you can begin on a gradual programme of increasing the intensity of the work, as well as the distance covered, as you get nearer to the time of the actual three-day event.

Plan how you intend to prepare for your first competition and work back from there. I divide my programme into three stages, which work out as slow work, build-up and sharpen-up, with the first part taking the longest and the latter part really being the last couple of weeks' fine tuning. Thereafter, you just maintain your horse to do whatever is planned.

There are basically two ways in which people prepare their horses for eventing. The first stage is the same for both, with between four and eight weeks being spent on the slow, hardening-up stage – the longer spent at this stage the better. At the second stage, riders can continue in the traditional method of a gradual build-up, increasing the work week by week, or start on interval training, whereby the horse is trained to do measured distances at set speeds with rest periods (intervals) in between. Both methods are well proven and have been equally successful, but the traditional method does rely on the rider having a certain amount of knowledge and feel, as well as experience, to be able to assess how the horse is progressing.

Interval training can be planned to create a specific programme for each horse, which is perhaps easier for the less-experienced rider to follow, knowing that the horse has a set programme of work. One difficulty that can crop up occasionally is whether the rider can assess if that programme is, in fact, making the horse work sufficiently.

SLOW WORK

This starts after the horse has been thoroughly checked over and shod. It should also have been wormed and had its teeth attended to recently. It should not have been allowed to get too fat and will probably start off looking well and rounded but not carrying excess weight. Should this be the case, the horse must be put on a strict diet as carrying excess weight on already soft legs is not a good beginning.

Introduce slow work by aiming for approximately 20–30 minutes on day one and finishing the week by doing one hour of walking. Watch the back and girth area for any signs of soreness. Harden the skin with surgical spirit if necessary. Sit lightly on your horse's back and do not ask for more than slight collection during the first week.

Progress slowly over the next week, to finish with two hours' walking with the horse carrying itself more. Weeks three and four can introduce a little slow trotting, initially for short periods and then gradually increasing a little. At this stage, a few hills can be introduced into your routes if this is possible. Do not overdo these or start by using very steep ones but gradually add them to your routes whenever possible.

Remember that road work can be jarring to the horse unless the trot is kept slow, which is when the horse will gain the maximum benefit. The slower the trot the more chance there is for the tendons and ligaments to stretch and contract with each stride, enabling maximum flexibility and toning up in those areas. Fast trotting is potentially harmful as it not only jars but also prevents the horse from using itself correctly as it is always in a tense, rather than a relaxed, state in which full extension and contraction of muscles are able to take place.

With any horse that has shown the slightest sign of tendon strain, I would continue building up, or maintaining, the road work phase from four to eight weeks, to give the legs a chance to harden really well. Thereafter, I would introduce the next phase, that of gradual schooling on the flat, two or three times a week after a half-hour hack to loosen the horse thoroughly.

The slow work period should never be considered boring by horse or rider as so much can be accomplished during this phase. The rider can work on loosening and softening the horse in the hand by bending the neck and body when possible. A little shoulder-in, renvers, travers, leg-yielding, half-halts and full halts can be carried out on a quiet road, and this will all go towards making your horse more supple and responsive and add variety to the work.

I like to do as much of the slow work as possible myself as it is during this time that you can develop muscle in the right or wrong places. If others do this phase for you, do be sure to explain quite clearly what you want done, otherwise many people will just slop along and 50 per cent of the value of this important phase will be lost. Week by week, a little more can be asked, always remembering to give adequate periods of stretching and relaxation for the stage of fitness. This is also a time to discover if a different bit might be more appropriate.

SCHOOLING

The second phase is the time when serious work can start but, again, you must introduce this gradually, by doing ten to twenty minutes or so at the end of a hack to start with, two to three times in the first week and then more often thereafter. Remember that it is canter that helps to fitten the cross country horse, as well as being the most important gait for the jumping horse. It seems to me that this is the gait *least* worked on by riders, which is half the reason why problems arise when it comes to jumping.

Schooling is essential to make your horse obedient to hand and leg. This horse is wearing a cheek snaffle and Grakle noseband – a popular combination for the stronger, slightly unresponsive horse.

If you cannot keep your horse in a steady rhythm and increase and decrease the pace without breaking into trot or meeting resistance, you should not be doing serious cross country anyway! Obedience is everything and your horse must be going forward into an even contact and respond to the slightest indication from your legs, whether you are asking for a forward movement or rebalancing.

Your flat work must include a lot of work on asking for impulsion then collection, which is so important in your approaches into the fences. You must also insist on obedience so that the transitions are soft and immediate, not resistant and in any old place. To be really successful, your horse must respond to your wishes instantly as if through a mutual understanding, as this will create the trust that makes truly great partnerships.

Schooling Exercises

Schooling is important as the degree to which the horse is trained will influence its performance dramatically. Some people spend hours on this and seem to achieve very little, while others appear to do the minimum but are very successful. As with everything, it is the quality of the work that counts. The eventer, in particular, has to be especially supple to cope with the different types of fence and terrain, as well as the different phases. Its work, therefore, must include as many suppling exercises, both on the flat and over fences, as possible. The following exercises include most of those that I find beneficial when schooling at home.

When schooling horses, it is very easy to forget the two essentials of all training: true straightness and ensuring that the horse is really going forward. Always ask yourself these two important questions as they affect everything the horse does. If these two essentials are not there, nothing can be achieved properly. Make sure you can really, honestly say that you are working the horse *forward* into a rounded or collected outline and not pulling it back to achieve collection. Every transition up or down must be a forward one – from leg into hand must be the general principle.

Loosen your horse up with a series of loops and circles before demanding anything too serious. Ask it to lengthen and shorten a little to really get it active and listening to you.

Work on transitions from one gait to another or from a medium to a collected pace and then on again to extended work in all gaits. Remember to keep your horse's interest by varying the work frequently. So often you hear the cry that the horse is heavy in the hand or leaning. This is

This rider is asking her horse to shorten from an extended canter to the more collected canter that is so essential for jumping.

hardly surprising when the majority of riders go round and round in circles endlessly pulling at their horse's head. The poor animal has no option other than to lean back unless enough is asked of it, through a series of half-halts and changes of pace and direction, to keep its balance back and off the forehand.

The halt is very useful and should be used much more than it is as a training aid. It is excellent for rebalancing the horse and, as every test starts and finishes with halt, it is the first and last impression that the judge has of you and your horse, and this certainly influences the marks given throughout the test. The horse should stand four square and should never step back but always be sent forward into the transition. It should also stand motionless and relaxed so, when doing halts, always take time for the horse to relax and think of this as a truly stationary movement. So much depends on the attitude of the rider and whether they sit still and stay relaxed. If the rider is tense, this usually percolates through to the horse who will fidget and move. Mentally relax yourself and breathe normally so that the horse does the same thing.

Straightness is the vital link in all work and is something that every rider must be constantly aware of throughout all training. If the horse is going correctly and being ridden forward, up to the bridle, it should be going straight. If its quarters are swinging, this usually means that it is not going forward or accepting the hand which is possibly being used too strongly. The same old problem then occurs, that of the rider trying to pull the horse back into a rounded outline instead of pushing it forward into a soft contact. Once it is no longer going forward, the horse will not be straight. Thereafter, all sorts of problems will develop through stiffness and evasion, which can lead to unlevelness and tension in all gaits.

Suppling exercises and strong forward movement will be required to put this problem right. Very often the horse will take hold of the bit on one side and/or tilt its head as it manoeuvres itself to one side or the other. By taking a stronger feel on the soft side and giving and releasing on the stiff side, you should be able to loosen the horse a little so long as forward impulsion is maintained. Keep varying the pace and try to work the horse through this stiffness. There is little point in asking for more collection until you have the horse obedient and going forward and straight, so keep your horse working on the basics until it feels really soft and obedient to your aids – then ask for more collection.

Collection and the various degrees of this are necessary before the horse can be asked to do anything too strenuous. Collection is really a redistribution of weight, demanding a higher degree of balance. Through schooling, the horse is able to 'carry itself' better, with its hind legs coming up more underneath it, closer to its centre of gravity. This is achieved by the horse being ridden with a strong seat and legs, enabling it to use its back and lower its quarters which, in turn, enables it to lighten and raise its forehand. The secret of collection is to ensure that this balance is achieved through the seat and legs and not by the reins.

Initially the horse will improve its balance through being ridden out on hacks, and going over uneven and undulating ground. In this way, it will learn to balance itself to a certain degree, which is the best way for a young horse to learn. As it matures, greater demands will be made on it by the rider, through careful schooling and by asking for more collection through changes of pace, increasing and decreasing the stride, suppling and lateral work, all achieved in a forward momentum but with more emphasis on the leg and seat aids.

Each gait will develop more active, higher strides as the horse's degree of collection improves, and it cannot be overstressed how important it is for the horse to be able to shorten and lengthen its stride in all gaits, particularly canter, as this affects your approach to the fences so much. In all schooling sessions some time must be spent on improving the canter and the obedience of the horse when responding to upward and downward transitions. By increasing collection, it is possible to push the centre of gravity further back and this can be vital when making adjustments on your approach to bigger fences.

The half-halt is one of the most useful methods of achieving balance and collection. It is literally what it says it is and is achieved through a redistribution of weight. The rider sits up and shortens the horse's stride through their seat, legs and hand, then drives it forward again, thereby creating a rebalancing effect which should be barely perceptible to the onlooker.

A series of half-halts is an excellent preparation in the early stages, when teaching the horse to halt square and correctly with its weight evenly distributed.

The circle is one of the classical schooling exercises and can vary in size from 20 m (66 ft) down to a volte of 6 m (19 ft). Circles are just as important for the jumping horse as they are for dressage and all horses should be able to turn equally well on either rein to perform circles in walk, trot or canter, as and when required. The horse's body should follow the curve of the circle, remaining on two tracks throughout and not allowing the quarters to swing out. The rider's weight must remain central, with the rider's hips in line with the quarters of the horse and the rider's shoulders following the curve of the circle, allowing the arms to dictate this – the inside rein indicates the direction, the outside one controls the degree of bend.

Half-circles on to the outside track from the centre line or from the three-quarter track will help to create better balance and control, and are a particularly useful exercise for making the horse use itself and come up off its forehand. For jumping, this exercise is invaluable but the horse must be capable of shortening and lengthening its stride with ease before it will cope well with the demands asked of it.

Bends and loops are excellent suppling exercises. They can be done through the correct use of corners, ensuring that the horse works into each corner, which then acts as a frequent rebalancing exercise. The horse has to increase the flexion in its body and joints to maintain its rhythm during the turns. Serpentines and loops on and off the track require the same effort. By starting with simple loops and building up to quite acute ones, you are asking the horse for extra balance and flexion.

Bends on and off the track can be done in trot or canter and serpentines can be done in canter, counter-canter or by using the changes of direction as a halt or walk balancing exercise before striking off on the other leg, all depending on the degree of schooling. The more exercises you can do, the more balanced and strong the horse will become.

Turns on the forehand and haunches are most useful to make the horse respond to the leg, and become loose and supple through its back, shoulder and quarters. These simple exercises are often forgotten yet can make an enormous difference to the looseness of the horse if done regularly. For the turn on the forehand, bring the horse to a square halt, then ask the quarters to move round into the school until the horse has done a complete half-circle round its forelegs and is facing the other way, then immediately move forwards.

For the turn on the haunches or half-pirouette, the opposite is required and the horse must execute a small semi-circle with its hind legs in a collected walk, bringing its head and forehand round to the inside until it is facing the other way. Neither movement should be hurried but the horse must take even steps round and sideways until it meets the track and then move forwards. Turn on the haunches is a continuous movement from walk, while turn on the forehand should start from halt.

For the more advanced rider, **lateral work** is probably the most useful means of suppling and loosening the horse and, depending on the horse's standard of training, this can start with shoulder-in, which all horses that are going forward, straight, in balance and with a rounded outline should be asked to do.

All schooling should be progressive and must aim at suppling the horse and making it more obedient to the rider's aids. Leg-yielding, shoulder-in and half-pass are excellent for this. Turns on the haunches and turns on the forehand (bringing the hind end round the forehand) are also very good for improving suppleness.

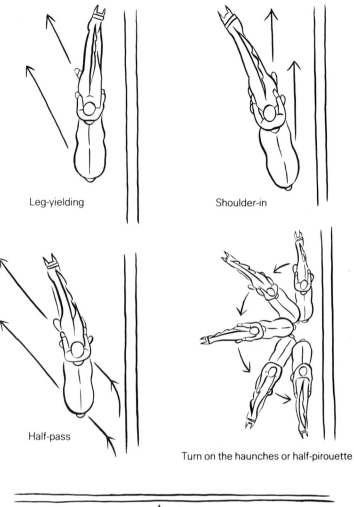

Leg-yielding

Shoulder-in

Half-pass

Turn on the haunches or half-pirouette

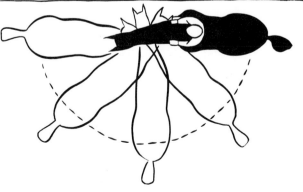

Turn on the forehand

Leg-yielding can be taught to ask the horse to move away from the leg. However, I am not in favour of this exercise if one is intending to teach half-pass later on as, in leg-yielding, the horse looks away from the direction in which it is going, while, for half-pass, it looks towards the direction in which it is going. I find this very confusing, both for the horse and when trying to train less experienced riders who then have to change their ideas completely if they want to achieve half-pass.

This rather exaggerated leg-yield looks as if it is being done rather fast, but it does demonstrate the extent of suppleness required, and also how much a horse can stretch and extend its legs, even when looking away from the direction of travel.

LEFT *A study in concentration as Vicky Latta of New Zealand takes Chief over the imposing obstacles at Gatcombe.*

BELOW *Mastering the technique required to negotiate various obstacles must be perfected early on in order to build up confidence for the bigger fences.*

RIGHT *Britain's Tanya Cleverly, on Watkins, sails over the huge box out of the Trout Hatchery on the homeward stretch at Burghley.*

BELOW *Schooling on the flat is essential to achieve those all-important low dressage marks. It also does much to improve the way the horse jumps across country and in the show jumping arena.*

LEFT *Germany's Herbert Blocker and the brilliant mare Feine Dame sail into the second water jump on the Barcelona course to win the Olympic bronze medal.*

BELOW *Even gold medallists have anxious moments! Matt Ryan shows all his brilliance in keeping his balance as he descends towards the water on his way to winning the gold medal for Australia. Kibah Tic Toc appears quite unconcerned!*

LEFT *Keeping up to time is essential on the roads and tracks phase, which can take you through wonderful countryside. The medical card required for British events is clearly seen on this rider's arm.*

BELOW *Schooling over grids is a wonderful way of teaching the horse to sort out its footwork and concentrate on what it is doing. It will also improve suppleness, balance and confidence.*

Natasha Wheeler jumps boldly through this attractive fence with an overhang before turning towards the water. Make sure that your horse is used to going through fences with 'lids' on as you are bound to encounter this type of fence and some horses are horrified by them!

THIS PAGE AND OPPOSITE *Jumping a combination downhill requires balance and control. If you go too fast, the horse will end up jumping too far out down the hill, which could jar it unnecessarily or cause a stumble, which might prove disastrous. Keep control and sit up.*

RIGHT *Getting horses used to water should start early and schooling sessions are advisable to ensure that, throughout its career, the horse remains confident about the variety of fences it may encounter at this type of obstacle.*

BELOW *Nearly everyone goes for at least one pre-season, cross country schooling round before going to their first event. This helps to get both the rider's and horse's eye in before competing, so that they are all set for success on the big day.*

LEFT *Shoulder-in is one of the most useful suppling exercises. Always be sure to allow your body to go with the horse rather than away from the forward movement.*

RIGHT *Half-pass is a natural progression from shoulder-in. Maintain the bend towards the direction in which you are going, by bending the horse around your inside leg and then push the horse away in that direction with your outside leg.*

Shoulder-in is a particularly useful movement when ridden up the track, on a circle or up the centre line. It influences balance and suppleness and helps to develop the rider's co-ordination. Start in walk up the track, asking for a bend through the shoulders to the inside with the inside leg forward on the girth, creating a bend to the inside. The outside rein controls the degree of bend and the outside leg prevents the quarters from swinging out. Never ask for too much bend to start with. Once the horse understands the exercise in walk, progress to trot but keep it slow and in balance.

Shoulder-in is the perfect base for teaching **half-pass**. After getting the bend up the long side of the school, all you need to do is to turn down the centre line, make a half-halt, maintain the bend back towards the track from which you have come and put your outside leg on to push the horse over in that direction. Remember that you must always be thinking of forward movement and this must always take priority over the sideways movement. When riding half-pass, I say to myself, 'Bend, forward, over; bend, forward, over', which helps to keep me thinking of the priorities. First of all get the bend, think forward, maintain this by keeping the inside leg forward on the girth, then push the horse over with the outside leg. If the horse is obedient to the aids, it should not find this difficult. Remember to sit up straight yourself and allow the horse to move over sideways without restricting its movement by the incorrect distribution of your own weight. You must go with the horse and not actively set yourself against the movement.

Counter-canter is another excellent exercise to help to create suppleness, co-ordination and balance, as it helps the tense horse, in particular, to loosen and relax. It should not be started in too small a space. Shallow loops off the track and back again are the best way to introduce the exercise. These can progress to deeper loops and, eventually, it should be possible to canter round the short track of the school in counter-canter.

If possible, practise circling in counter-canter in an open space to start with, so that you can give the horse all the room it needs if it finds this difficult. A well-balanced, obedient horse usually finds this exercise quite easy. Very often the true canter and trot rhythm will improve considerably after a few minutes in counter-canter.

Collected canter is one of the most important paces for the jumping horse as it can dramatically affect the way the horse jumps. Counter-canter and changes into and out of this, plus increasing and decreasing the pace on frequent occasions, will all help towards the creation of a good canter.

THE IMPORTANCE OF A CORRECT WARM-UP AND COOL-DOWN

One aspect of training which seems seriously neglected by many riders is the importance of a proper warming-up period before commencing serious work or at a competition, as well as that of cooling the horse down after work.

No athlete ever comes straight on to the track to run; they spend a lot of time loosening and limbering up their muscles, and can be seen doing numerous exercises to ensure that every muscle is warm, loose, in good working order and ready for the demands about to be made on it.

All too often, the horse is taken from its stable where it has spent the last 22 hours or so cooped up and, within a few minutes, can be seen working in a school on the bit, often being asked to extend, circle or collect itself before it has had a chance to loosen up. This hurried approach to work can lead to tension and stiffness, not to mention the physical danger of attempting anything before the circulation is fully active.

The importance of loosening the horse up slowly before work cannot be overemphasized. This rider is asking for a lower outline to start with, before asking the horse to carry its head more and work through from behind.

At the end of a work session, it is equally important to allow the horse to relax, which promotes both physical and mental well-being.

An eminent vet once said to me that, in his opinion, more damage was done to horses' legs by people with their own manèges, who brought their horse straight out of the stable into the school and started work before giving the horse a chance to loosen up. He genuinely felt that every stabled horse should have an absolute minimum period of 15 minutes' walking on a firm surface before starting anything, particularly in schools where the artificial surfaces make extra demands on the horse which is accustomed to moving on *terra firma* in its natural state.

Since then, I have always insisted that our horses go for a walk or hack before coming into the school to work or jump seriously. Over the years I have been extremely fortunate in having incurred only a few training injuries and am sure that this advice has helped enormously.

Cooling the horse down after work or a gallop is equally important as the lactic acid build-up in the muscles, following anaerobic exercise, can cause stiffness. Although, during most training sessions, the horse should not reach this state except during galloping or jumping, stiffness can still occur if it is not given adequate time to relax mentally and physically, and to unwind before being confined to its stable again. By their very nature, conformation or former history, some horses are more prone to stiffness than others. If these horses need more time to loosen up or to relax after work, then they should be given this time.

Some people are able to turn their horses out more than others. If this is possible, either before or after work, or both, it is definitely in the best interests of most horses. Some people have horse walkers and these are excellent for this purpose, especially in a yard where there are a lot of horses and there is simply not time to give every horse the ideal start or finish to its work. Riding and leading can work well if you send off a couple of horses for a walk while you ride others, or send a helper off for a hack on one and then school it when it comes back, then send your long-suffering helper off on the other to cool it down! There are numerous ways in which such things can be done if time is short.

Whatever you do, remember that all horses and riders need time to become motivated, both physically as well as mentally. Allowing sufficient time to warm up well, to work in before a test, to prepare for your jumping or cross country round will pay off in having a relaxed and more responsive horse. Likewise, if you can allow the horse enough time to unwind and relax afterwards, it is likely to think of work or competing as nothing more than an ordinary job to be done, and will take it much more in its stride than one that is rushed from the outset and then chucked back into the box afterwards to worry and fret about what is coming next!

PLANNING THE THIRD STAGE

It is during the schooling phase that you should be looking ahead and introducing some slow, but steady, faster work and there are two main ways of doing this. First, through the old, traditional method, introducing a bit of cantering gradually over the following five to six weeks, increasing the distance and then the speed as the horse becomes fitter. The second method is interval training (see p.80).

Traditional Fitness Programme

The traditional method, of gradually increasing fast work week by week, requires considerable experience and knowledge so that the horse is worked through 'feel' rather than to a set programme. The same basic build-up of slow work and conditioning is practised as for interval training. Thereafter, slow cantering should start once a week, later increasing to twice a week, depending on the horse.

The speed is kept relatively slow (half speed), with a faster finishing speed (three-quarter speed) for the last 800–1,200 m (½–¾ miles). The horse is never fully extended and is always held well together and up to the bit. A good rhythm is essential and the horse must work in a calm and relaxed way. The rider generally works with a watch, increasing the time a little on each occasion. Alternatively, if you have a variety of rides, where you can canter or gallop on good ground, increasing the distance over time is an easy way to progress. Beginning with five minutes in the first week and increasing over the next month to 15–20 minutes is normal practice.

The horse should never go flat out at any time but must remain obedient to the rider's aids and maintain a steady, relentless canter where the ground permits. If the terrain is very flat, you should not hammer your horse's legs by going too fast but must maintain a steady rhythm throughout. Always start slowly, let the horse establish its rhythm and then ask for a more positive stride. Ideally, push on up a slight hill for the last 400–800 m (¼–½ miles), so that the horse starts to develop its respiratory system, but do not put this under too much stress too soon. Increase speed and distance week by week.

Good stable management is essential and the rider must be vigilant in checking for heat, swelling or signs of overwork. If any of these occur you must cut back for a few days until it has settled. This training system is very flexible and how you train, and where, can be adapted to suit all types of horses' temperaments.

The chart opposite offers a guide as to the programme that might be adopted by those aiming for a Novice, Intermediate or Advanced three-day event. (For those doing one-day events at this standard, the relevant part can be used as a guide.) Everyone has different methods or ideas but it is the basics that require the most time in early training; thereafter, your schedule can be made flexible to include all the different training sessions necessary for the event horse. Remember that a horse that is getting fit for the first time will usually take longer than on subsequent occasions.

FITNESS GUIDE FOR NOVICE ONE-DAY EVENT

Weeks	
1–2	Road work – walking for ¾ to 1½ hours
3–4	Road work – walking and slow trotting for 1½–2 hours
5–6	Road work – hacking and schooling on the flat
7–8	Slow cantering, hacking, road work and grid work
9–10	As above, plus cross country schooling and one gallop per week
11–12	Novice one-day event

FITNESS GUIDE FOR INTERMEDIATE THREE-DAY EVENT

As above to weeks 9–10. Attend intermediate events 2–3 weeks apart as necessary.

Weeks	
11–12	Cross country schooling, show jumping and 1–2 gallops 4–6 weeks apart. Attend last one-day event 2–3 weeks before three-day event
End of weeks 12–14	Intermediate three-day event

FITNESS GUIDE FOR ADVANCED THREE-DAY EVENT

As above to weeks 10–12

Weeks	
13–14	Long hacks, schooling in all phases. Attend a competition
15–18	Fast work and/or 1 or 2 competitions
18–19	Three-day event

Interval Training

Interval training is very popular among event riders as it aims to develop the horse's ability to work over longer periods of time without a build-up of lactic acid in the muscles, which is one of the major contributory factors to the onset of fatigue.

The idea is to give measured periods of work followed by a short period of rest (interval) during which the horse only partly recovers before it is asked to work again. It is most important that this training method is not begun until the horse has had at least six or seven weeks' slow conditioning work to harden up legs, back and muscles in readiness for competitive work. Thereafter, you will train over set distances in a set time.

For general fittening work, three work periods and two rest periods are the normal pattern, increasing the time and the speed as time goes by and, eventually, decreasing the length of the rest intervals. For more strenuous work, such as fittening for a three-day event, many people increase the schedule to five work periods and four rest intervals. A programme should be devised to suit each individual horse and the training is normally carried out every four to five days.

It is important to monitor the horse's progress throughout by taking pulse and respiration readings so that you can assess how the horse is coping with the work and whether there are any problems with what you are doing. If the horse finds your programme a bit too much, you must back off a little, cut back on your work periods and then build up again over a couple of weeks.

It is essential that the horse is in good general condition before starting this training and that it is already finding the slow work quite easy. Remember that the horse's response to hot or humid weather will affect how it copes. Its breathing may become more rapid or it may take longer to return to normal as the horse's system works to cool it down. The pulse is generally less affected, except in extreme conditions. The horse's recovery rate is the main element in this form of training and the quicker it recovers from progressive work, the fitter it is likely to be.

Most horses respond well to interval training and it is an excellent way of ensuring that the horse gets enough work in preparation for whatever it is going to be asked to do, so long as a realistic schedule has been worked out to begin with. Occasionally, one will find a horse that becomes overexcited by the regimentation of this system, or that does not work hard enough if it is a lazy sort, and these horses may do better on the traditional fitness system. You can also vary your work between interval training sessions, to include dressage and jumping schooling as well as hillwork if this is available to you.

Always give the horse light work on the day after your workouts, just as you would after a competition, or turn it out or lead it out for a rest day once a week. If you compete or go for cross country schooling, this will count as a work day, so you will need only one interval training session that week. Be flexible in your programme, so that the horse is not overtaxed.

Method Interval training is usually begun around the sixth to seventh week. For this, a good start would be three three-minute canters at around 350 metres per minute (mpm), which could then be increased over the next fortnight to three four-minute canters at 400 mpm. Interval training is usually carried out twice a week with other work slotted into the programme in between. Everyone has their own method of devising a programme for each horse but the important thing is to study your

This rider is checking her watch during her interval training workout. The distance and speed will gradually be increased as the horse becomes fitter.

horse's progress and adjust the work to suit its stage of fitness. The work sessions should gradually increase in intensity and the rest periods (intervals) should decrease slightly. The horse should be able to do three five-minute canters at 450 mpm, with the last of these increasing to 500–600 mpm, just before the event you are working towards.

Faster periods of work, especially the last one of the three mentioned above, will help to stress the respiratory system and develop greater tolerance to faster work. The horse should find the work easy and its recovery rate (the time taken for its breathing rate to return to relative normality) should improve with each workout. It is good if the horse blows hard but you must be certain as to how quickly it is starting to recover and make sure that this is also taking less and less time.

The horse should not be overgalloped but neither should it be underworked at the faster pace if it is going to a three-day event or doing Advanced one-day eventing or team chasing as it will need to be fit to jump round a course of a minimum of 4 km (2½ miles) fairly fast, depending on the standard. For eventing this speed varies between 520–600 mpm on the cross country. In the steeplechase phase in a three-day event, it varies from 640–690 mpm.

Once fit, the horse only requires enough work to maintain that level. Generally, the events themselves will work towards keeping up the fitness level and the horse will require less work. Remember that relaxation and rest are as important as the work and that it is easy to overdo things. The horse is entitled to a few days off every now and then, and turning it out will help to relax it, especially if it is a rather tense and up-tight sort of horse. Unless it goes out every day, keep an eye on its legs in case it knocks itself. I always put brushing boots on if the horse only goes out occasionally. Accidents can occur if the horse gallops around a lot, so it is usually best to turn it out in a small paddock. If a quiet horse, that does not gallop, is turned out with your fit one, this sometimes helps to keep the fit horse quiet.

The event horse must be fit enough to gallop at the necessary speed for the standard of the competition. In a three-day event the steeplechase is usually the most demanding section for the horse's legs because it is the fastest phase. However, the fences and ground on the cross country course are very demanding so the horses must be very fit.

THE IMPORTANCE OF BALANCE AND RHYTHM

I cannot overstress how important it is to train the horse to work in balance and in a good, even rhythm. This becomes even more essential at three-day events where the more relaxed the horse can be kept, the less likelihood there will be of it taking too much out of itself unnecessarily. Every bit of energy saved will help the horse to a better performance.

Keeping the horse balanced between your leg and hand makes all the difference in competition, and this will be so much easier if you are confident that you can lengthen and shorten the stride as required as a result of careful training on the flat. When doing your fast work, practise moving the horse on and then bringing it back so that it becomes second nature for it to do this at speed. If you need to rebalance at any time during a competition, you will then be able to do so with confidence, knowing that the horse will respond quickly. If your horse is obedient about doing this when training for fast work, it will be much more willing to do so on your cross country schooling rounds.

The degree of training you achieve on the flat will make all the difference to how you cope with jumping. This rider is working on maintaining a rhythm and being able to shorten and lengthen the horse's strides.

4

POLE WORK
AND JUMP TRAINING

POLE EXERCISES AND IMPROVING ATHLETIC ABILITY

The use of poles to help the horse to become more athletic and supple, and to give variation to everyday schooling is, I believe, invaluable. This becomes particularly true for those people who have to rely excessively on indoor and outdoor schools and do not have unlimited riding in the countryside. So much can be learnt while out hacking, without the horse even realizing how it is having continually to adjust its balance and weight to cope with variations in the terrain or conditions.

The sooner the young horse is introduced to poles, the better but, for all horses, poles can be used to loosen and supple them in numerous ways, whether going over, round or through them.

If you have a helper, poles can be varied but they are generally set at around 1.3 m (4ft 6 in) for the average horse's stride in trot. As I am often alone, I find setting them at about double this (3 m or nearly 10 ft) is a more useful distance. The horse can then walk, trot or canter through poles set like this. In walk and trot the horse will put a stride in between each pole; in canter it should make a stride over each pole if a good steady rhythm is maintained.

Each horse will have a slightly different length of stride and, especially over poles set at 1.3 m (4 ft 6 in) for trotting, it is important that these are adjusted to suit that particular horse's stride. If alone, you could set the poles on a semi-circle or fan shape, which can then be ridden over at the distance that is comfortable for your horse. This will also encourage your horse to work a little harder as it will have to stretch a little on the outside and flex its joints a little more on the inside.

For the short-striding horse, riding over poles on a circle will encourage it to lengthen its stride if you can keep it a little to the outside of its normal striding.

ABOVE *This horse is demonstrating how work over poles requires greater effort and therefore a greater degree of suppleness. To receive the maximum benefit, the horse must lower its head and loosen its back muscles.*

Circling through poles is excellent for suppling and for concentrating the mind of a horse that tends to look around a lot or is always in a hurry. Vary your work to include work over the poles in a series of twists and turns. For these to be really versatile, poles set at 3 m (about 10 ft) are best. The following exercises are ones I use a lot but you can make up different versions as you go along. The horse needs to be relaxed and settled before any real benefit is felt when using poles. It must also be remembered that the horse has to work considerably harder over poles, with higher, more active steps, so care must be taken not to overtire the horse in the early stages. Raised trotting poles require even more effort.

BELOW *The value of circling over, through and around poles cannot be overestimated. It teaches the horse to think and respond as well as to relax, which all help when it comes to the jumping phases.*

I always start by walking through the poles or circling round each one in turn until the horse has settled. The exuberant horse may liven up on seeing the row of poles, so confuse it a bit by trotting down through the middle of them, then circling down over one to the left, the next to the right, then to the left, etc. This will usually settle the horse quite quickly if started in walk.

Other variations include making a serpentine round the ends of each pole, starting in walk and then progressing to trot. A young or green horse may need to miss out a pole if the turns come a bit too quickly.

Poles provide an excellent method of loosening and suppling horses of all ages and standards. It is possible to go over, around and through poles in numerous different ways, as shown. A distance of 1.3 m (4 ft 6 in) is generally about right for trotting; 3 m (10 ft) is about average for cantering or for putting one stride between each pole.

Trotting poles set at
1.3 m (4 ft 6 in) or 3 m (10 ft)

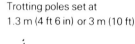

Set distance in middle
at 1.3 m (4 ft 6 in)

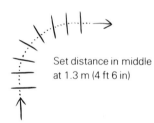

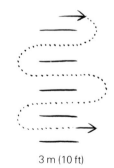

3 m (10 ft)

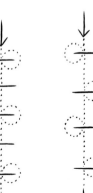

3 m (10 ft)   3 m (10 ft)

Trotting a circle over the first two poles and then going on down, circling in the opposite direction over each one or two poles and varying what you do is useful. Trotting down and stopping midway is also good for co-ordination, obedience and balance. Walking over two poles, then trotting the next two or three, then walking again is also excellent for balance and co-ordination as well as obedience.

Trotting straight down through the poles before, during or after any of these exercises helps to improve rhythm so long as you consciously think of maintaining this. Because the horse takes a full stride between each pole, change the diagonal frequently so that you are not always working on the same one because some horses will then organize themselves to meet the poles on a specific diagonal.

Cantering down through the poles can be a very useful exercise for the short-striding horse or one that tends not to go forward well, but it is not recommended for one that gets overexcited, although, with some, the poles will, in fact, slow them down. Experiment and see. Usually you can see after two or three tries if something is going to get better or worse.

Circling over two poles in canter can be very good for the over-enthusiastic horse. Cantering down and walking or halting over a specific pole and then going on again is also excellent. One really good exercise is that of circling round a pole or two poles, that are set in line, in canter. This helps your horse to balance itself and stay in rhythm.

Start by circling round two poles, or even three if your horse is young or green, and then come down to two or one if it can cope. First establish your canter, get the horse listening to you and canter a few circles round the school, then work in between the poles and circle round them every now and then. I find this a most useful way of making the horse obedient and supple, and the canter very quickly begins to improve as rhythm and balance start to create a better pace.

GRID WORK

Grids can be enormously beneficial to the horse's overall schooling, helping to promote good balance and teaching the horse to think for itself. The best use of a grid is for setting the horse different striding problems using a variety of fences and poles set in a straight line. Uprights, bounces and spreads can be incorporated into the grid, which should start as a fairly simple affair and then develop into a more serious exercise as the horse learns how to cope with the demands.

To make a grid really beneficial, the rider should leave as much as possible to the horse but must remain in trot and in balance throughout, never getting in front of the movement nor left behind it, and enabling the horse to shorten or lengthen its stride as necessary. A cross pole is the ideal start to the grid, usually with a placing pole 2–3 m (6½–10 ft) in front of it to encourage the horse to take off at the right place. This fence can then be built up, incorporating a placing pole at around 3 m (about 10 ft). This could be followed by an upright or bounce, a couple of poles on the ground and then a spread. A pole on the landing side at a distance of 3 m (10 ft) will encourage the horse to stretch and look down, thereby influencing it to round over its fences.

The initial, high cross pole will encourage the horse to be neat in front and to fold its forelegs. These are very beneficial for a horse that tends to dangle its front legs and can be used frequently in your grid in place of a straight rail. Double cross rails will also encourage the horse to round more over its fences as well as being neat in front. They should not

Although this cross pole is small, the rider is working on giving the horse sufficient freedom over the fence and on maintaining a good, active trot, which will be essential when it comes to the more awkward cross country fences.

be used until the horse is confident and quite experienced in going through grids, however, as the effect of so many poles can be a little daunting and the horse may start to back off from the fence. Jump one or two as a single fence before incorporating them into a grid.

Parallels encourage roundness as well as forcing the horse to make an effort to stretch over the fence and so build up power. To start with, have one at the end of your grid, with a pole afterwards, at a distance of 3 m (about 10 ft) to help the horse to stretch down over the fence and then rebalance itself over this pole a stride after landing.

Keep the parallels small to start with, especially with a young horse and increase first the width, then gradually the height. For the experienced horse, you can incorporate parallels throughout the grid so that the horse is encouraged to stretch, then shorten, then stretch again. By using an upright or high cross after a spread, the horse is encouraged

This horse is jumping a grid, starting with poles on the ground leading to a small parallel followed by another pole on the ground. It is picking its forelegs up very neatly and clearing the height easily.

to adjust its weight (likewise if a bounce is used) and such exercises will help to teach the horse to back off from its fences and think for itself.

The rider can help by sitting up over the placing pole and then following through over the fence. The use of body weight can be very helpful if used correctly to balance the horse, but can also be the downfall of many if used in the wrong way. If the rider stays forward all the time, the horse may be encouraged to rush and go on to its forehand, so that it is never very neat in front. Too great a shift in the rider's body weight can unbalance the horse and be such a hindrance that it hits the fences both behind and in front. Aim to sit up over the poles on the ground, using your weight and legs to balance rather than allowing your hands to pull on the reins. Keep your lower leg firmly on the horse and stay in balance with it, following its movement over each fence.

Grids should not be overdone – once or twice a week is ample for most horses – but they are very useful for the event horse which has to cope with so many different problems when going cross country. They help to keep the rider's mind sharp and the horse supple and athletic. Grids will also assist in building up muscle power. Vary your grids regularly so that there is a different problem for the horse to assess each time. Once the horse has learnt how to cope, nothing will be gained from endlessly repeating the same exercise, although the occasional repeat will keep it sharp and alert.

Developing the Canter

The rhythm of the canter and the pace in which you approach the fences are important factors. If you do not have a steady rhythm, it will be very difficult to assess your striding into the obstacle. If you have too much or too little pace, you will be in danger of knocking down the fence and undermining the horse's confidence.

Spend plenty of time on your canter work, as this affects all your jumping work, both in the arena and out on the cross country course. Your horse must be obedient to your leg aids and you must be able to maintain the canter throughout, so that you do not lose vital impulsion on the approach. If your horse finds it difficult to keep a steady rhythm in canter, ride it on a circle over a parallel several times until you can really keep up a rhythm and maintain an even stride. Do this again on the other rein and as frequently as is needed until you feel confident you can keep your horse balanced in canter over fences.

When it comes to cross country riding, you then only have to increase the pace a bit more, pushing the horse more into the hand.

However, this increase in pace can result in the horse becoming a little too onward-bound and strong in the hand in some cases. Therefore obedience training, which should ensure that the horse will respect your demands, is essential.

Being able to increase and decrease the pace, so that you can ride on or bring the horse back when required, makes for a confident partnership. It should be possible to achieve this with ease with a more obedient horse but for those that become overstrong, it may be necessary to review the braking system and try a different bit.

The flying change is an essential exercise that should be mastered by all jumping riders. It is not difficult to do as a jumping exercise and can be taught with or without a pole as a useful aid. If using a pole, place this on the long diagonal in the middle of the school, establish a good canter and come across the diagonal towards the pole. As you approach, prepare with a half-halt, change your leg aids quite strongly and ask for a different bend to the inside. As the horse jumps across the pole, emphasize the movement with a change of your body weight towards the inside at the same time. Once you can do this with the horse changing legs over the pole, it should soon be possible to do the same without a pole, simply by being positive with your aids and making sure the horse is listening to you.

To teach flying change without a pole is equally easy if the horse is going well on the flat and is obedient to the leg aids. Prepare for the movement with a half-halt and ask for the change in a suitable place, such as in the corner following a loop back or change of rein, across the diagonal or over the centre line when doing a serpentine.

If the horse is not so well schooled, it is still possible to do a flying change by exaggerating the use of your aids. When asking the horse to change, really take the rein on the near side and really use your offside leg to 'kick' the horse on to the other diagonal. Shifting your body weight towards the new leading leg as the horse changes during the moment of suspension will help as well.

So many nice rounds are spoilt by riders losing rhythm as they pull back to a trot to change on to the right leg instead of doing a flying change. It can save seconds in a jump-off and is not a problem if you learn how to do it properly in the first place. Alternatively, it is quite easy to keep going on the wrong leg as long as you maintain a good rhythm and keep the horse balanced throughout turns and going towards the fences. This is often better than failing to do a change or losing the canter and falling into trot.

JUMPING A COURSE

Once the horse has learnt how to be neat and athletic through grids, the next stage is to be confident about jumping round a course of fences if the horse has not already done this. Nowadays, many equestrian centres run clear-round jumping competitions at different levels and if this is available to you, I cannot think of a better schooling facility. You have the competitive atmosphere, a variety of fences and can begin at whatever height you wish by appearing at the right time. With a young horse, it is perhaps best to start over a smaller course than you have practised on at home. The youngster is bound to be a bit overawed by the outing and an easy few rounds on your first couple of visits will ensure a build-up of confidence for the future.

For the experienced horse, coming along for a practice round after a lay-off or at the beginning of the season, this is the ideal time to try out new techniques or bits, or just to get your eye in before a more serious

America's Nancy Bliss looking for her next fence – important when aiming for a good clear round in the jumping phase. Accuracy on approach and a good line to each obstacle are vital to success.

Too often the show jumping lets people down. It is as important to practise this in the atmosphere of a proper competition as it is to school at home. Go to as many show jumping competitions as you can if you want to be a successful event rider. (William Fox Pitt on Chaka at Badminton.)

competition. Every rider/horse combination benefits from a warm-up outing before the real thing. Not only does it help to sharpen up the rider, it also serves to settle the horse. These outings are also invaluable if your horse has suffered a setback and needs to go down a slot to regain confidence following a disaster.

If such facilities are not available, you will need to get a little more organized at home and arrange to jump a series of fences when schooling. Build four or five jumps that can be taken from either direction and site these in such a way that you can flow on as if on a course. If you have a wall, gate and brightly coloured fillers, so much the better, as the horse will then become quite used to these before it meets them at a competition.

For a spooky horse, you can improvise by draping a coat or coloured rug over a small fence and then ride positively at it, not standing for any nonsense. Sheets of plastic can be laid under a fence to look like water. Make sure, however, that this does not flap around, either by lying a pole on top of it on both sides if it is less than 1 m (3 ft 3 in) wide, or by pinning it down safely. Your aim should be to encourage the horse to jump unusual fences, not to frighten it to death, so never try jumping anything too big until the horse is confident about spooky fences set up at home! Some older horses are occasionally quite silly about spooks and may need firm encouragement if they are being naughty. My Badminton horse was horrified when I placed a small fence in front of a big puddle and refused to jump it for ages, yet she sailed into the daunting lake fence at Badminton, which she presumably felt was a proper obstacle!

If you have an Advanced horse, you will be required to jump over water trays or water at one-day or three-day events, so be sure you practise over a proper water jump beforehand. For a water jump, you require the horse to jump up as well as out, so practise first with a brush or something similar in front of it, and also place a pole over the middle of the water to teach the horse to come up over these fences rather than to jump flat over them and risk going in, which is very costly.

Show jumping water jumps are not too easy to find but it really is worth making the effort to go and school over one before being confronted by one in competition. Many people do not bother to do this, only to be eliminated on the third day of the event because their horse was horrified to see a water jump full of blue dye, or whatever, which came as a complete surprise in the show jumping round. Do not take this risk as, once a horse has stopped and been eliminated in competition, it soon learns that it can get to stop after three tries when you have to leave the ring. An intelligent horse may never be reliable again once it has learnt that this can be the easy way home.

Combinations need practice and should vary in their striding. A one- and two-stride double, with every combination of jumps, should be practised: vertical to spread, vertical to vertical, spread to vertical, spread to spread, etc., then add an extra fence to make a treble and, again, vary the fences. Also slightly shorten or lengthen the strides in between so

Water jumps will be found at all Advanced-standard competitions. Accustom your horse to these well in advance, so that it knows what to expect and how to stretch out over them.

that you know your horse will be able to cope with any reasonable striding if you ride it accordingly. It is just as important that the rider knows how to cope as well as the horse, so keep your own eye sharp and your responses quick.

Having ensured that all aspects of the jumps themselves have been thoroughly mastered and that the horse appears happy to jump all types of obstacles confidently, you must then work on fluency and rhythm over your course, so that the whole performance seems easy and is pleasing to watch.

TRAINING FOR THE STEEPLECHASE PHASE (PHASE B)

Steeplechase training is just as important as that for cross country but will not require more than two or three practice sessions in most cases. In the steeplechase phase the horse is required to jump faster and less carefully over the top of each fence. It can slightly brush through the top but must not waste time in the air when doing so. You need to ride with shorter stirrups and be well braced against the horse so that you remain in control at this faster speed.

If you have no suitable fences of your own, the best way to practise for the steeplechase is to find out where your nearest trainer is and approach them to see if you can go and use the fences. Respect the ground and ask if there is anywhere the trainer does not want you to ride. Most trainers are very strict about keeping their gallops in the best possible condition and riding on them in the wrong direction can cause a problem in some areas unless hoofprints are trodden in properly. You might even be able to persuade the trainer to come and give you some valuable advice on your style and technique.

Some horses take to steeplechasing very well, establish a good stride and settle quickly into a rhythm. Others tend to slow up when coming into the fences, which not only loses the rhythm but also reduces the speed. For such horses, a couple of sessions alongside a more experienced horse, galloping stride for stride, usually helps. Keep your leg on firmly, offer a firm support with the reins and then encourage the horse away from the fence after the jump so that it keeps up a steady, relentless gallop at the speed in which you are aiming to compete.

Some horses go the other way and become too strong when steeplechasing, requiring a change of the braking system. This may only be the addition of a flash noseband or it may be a different bit. Something that does not encourage the horse to lean too much and bear down, such as one of the roller snaffles or a mild gag to bring the head up, may be the answer. Control is essential, however, and this needs to be sorted out *before* you get to the competition. Sometimes a gag works well on the steeplechase and then you can change the reins on to the main bit rings for the cross country phase, when the horse is more settled. Remember that sometimes more in the mouth makes the horse worse and it may be speeding up to avoid pain, so that, in some cases, it might go better in a milder bit. Assess how you use your hands. Again, the horse could be running away from a hard hand and a softer, more sympathetic approach may be all that is needed. Other horses, however, might take advantage of this moment to really take off and run away, so you need to be certain you have mastered the brakes before chancing the steeplechase phase.

Timing

To practise the speeds for the different standards of competition, you are best to adopt the principle of riding over a measured distance at the necessary pace. Proper gallops have furlong posts as this is the standard racing measurement, but you will also need to work out how fast you should be over a kilometre at your necessary speed and then get the feel of that with your particular horse. Some horses really lengthen their stride in gallop and are easy to assess, while others find it more difficult to establish a rhythm or are very sensitive to the ground, shortening their stride dramatically in firm conditions.

It is important that you know how your horse will react to the different ground conditions so that you can work out how to ride your course overall. With a horse that is on the slow side or a bit short of class, it may be best to risk a few time penalties on the steeplechase phase so that it still has enough stamina in reserve to do the cross country at a reasonable speed.

The steeplechase fences can look quite daunting to some horses, so do not get caught out if your horse slows down to look – kick on firmly and keep the horse up together, going forward well. If this is a problem, practise a few times alongside another horse to encourage yours to go forward, lengthen its stride and gallop in a rhythm at the right speed for what is required.

Cross Country Jumping Techniques

If your horse is used to all the different types of questions asked on a cross country course, you are likely to encounter very few problems. Training for every type of fence should be done at home or when

schooling for cross country so that the horse is not surprised on the day. Although there are numerous variations of the main cross country fences, it is important that the horse is confident about how to cope with the basic types at cross country speed.

Upright fences rarely cause problems as long as you approach in a steady rhythm with the horse held well between hand and leg, and let the fence come to the horse. Remain in balance at all times and approach each fence at a sensible pace, depending on its position.

Spreads require a little more effort to clear the width as well as the height. Do not be encouraged to take off too far away. Generally come straight at them, especially on young horses, only coming at an angle to those that demand it and once your horse is experienced enough. Fences such as footbridges require a very accurate line and good forward rhythm so that the horse has an easy jump. Once on your line, really ride forward so that the horse jumps out well and makes a good getaway on the other side. Spreads with a drop landing need to be ridden at steadily on the initial approach but you must then really give the horse its head over the fence and bring the head up to rebalance the horse on landing.

Angled fences require accuracy and demand a forward approach. It is no good weaving about at these; you must get on to your line and then ride forward. If these have been practised often enough when schooling, they should present few problems. If the horse tends to duck out to one side or the other, there is usually a reason for this. Is it going forward between hand and leg? Is it dropping the bit and hanging to one side because it is uncomfortable in its mouth? There is likely to be a simple answer, which can be dealt with if you are fully aware of the problem. The important point is to put this right as soon as possible before it develops into a bad habit that can easily wreck a horse's reputation.

Certain exercises can help to cure this form of running out, such as riding over single fences at an angle from different directions and aiming to jump only over the centre. Think positively yourself and ride on a definite line from a certain point before the fence to a certain point beyond it.

Ian Stark makes nothing of the big spread when jumping the Whitbread Drays. This type of fence should be jumped straight to ensure that it is not made any wider for the horse to jump.

You can also place two, then three, fences in a line but set on the diagonal, with three strides between them, then two, then one. Ride straight through. Keep the horse going forward strongly between hand and leg.

Some horses tend to duck out or hang to one side, which makes these close-set fences a problem. Check that your bitting is not too severe and that you are not stronger with one hand than the other so that the horse is not trying to get away from your hand. Keep an even feel on the reins and look and ride straight towards your goal.

Occasionally, you will meet a series of fences that require the horse to turn in the air slightly to meet each on an angle. Using your inside rein is essential here and all riders should be competent at taking the rein away from the neck towards the direction in which they are travelling. Do not restrict the degree of bend by fixing the outside rein on the neck. This will defeat the object of the exercise as the horse cannot then turn at all. Practise approaching parallels set at an angle and landing each time on a different leg so that you ride a figure of eight.

Corners require precision riding, so most of the same principles apply. Accuracy is everything. There are so many different designs of corner that it is imperative you can trust your horse at these fences and be confident that it will go straight and stay on your chosen line of approach. Always look for a point in front of the fence and then line this up with an obvious point (tree etc) after the fence so that your line will take you over the part of the corner you wish to jump. Once you get on to this line, do not steady the horse excessively or it will start to waver – keep it balanced and in a steady rhythm, then ride on and straight over the fence.

Corners can be built quite easily at home in the schooling area. Barrels make excellent ends as they are rounded and unlikely to injure the horse should it 'glance off'. Start with a narrow corner, especially for a youngster and then, over a few sessions, you can widen this out. Remember to change your approach if the angle demands it as you can only come at it straight if you have widened both the back and front poles equally.

Remember the principle behind riding a corner – dissect the point with an imaginary line down the centre – it is this line that you jump straight, not the front or back rail. Some corners are quite narrow so use shorter poles occasionally to get the horse accustomed to these.

If you have a horse that tends to run out, you will have to start from the beginning and teach it what you expect of it. Place a pole on the edge of the apex to hold the horse to its line and then, when it has jumped the fence correctly a few times, remove this. You may need to do this on two or three occasions until you feel confident that you have got it right. Horses quickly learn how to do things if they are taught correctly from the beginning. However, they equally quickly learn how to *avoid* doing things, so it is worth getting this right before meeting it in competitions.

A good jump over this corner makes it all look so easy. It is most important to walk your line beforehand. Remembering to keep to your chosen approach to the fence is vital for a safe jump.

Arrowheads are increasingly being used on courses and, once again, the emphasis is on accuracy and obedience. Can you keep your horse straight on a line over narrow fences? This, again, can be practised in your schooling area if you can find a couple of short poles. We cut our broken ones up into 1.5-m (5-ft), 122-cm (4-ft) and 91-cm (3-ft) lengths, and then use them to school over. To be effective, you require jump stands that are short, narrow, single ones, so that they will not act as too much of a wing.

I begin to train my horses for arrowheads by leaning two poles against the fence stands to guide the horse into the channel. Keep the jump low to start with as it looks rather off-putting. Once the horses have jumped this confidently, I place the guide poles on the floor and then, later, take them away altogether.

Thereafter, you can practise over two fences in a row, with one or two strides between them. Get on to your line and hold your horse straight between hand and leg. Such fences really do demand accuracy and it is very important that you get narrow fences lined up carefully so that the horse is able to see them as two obvious jumps. All too often you see mistakes being made because the rider has not paid enough attention to the approach and has not given the horse sufficient time to see what is coming up.

Sometimes you will come across arrowheads following a drop landing and, for these, the rider must be quick to react after the drop to keep the horse straight for the arrowhead. A safe, secure leg position is vital for the rider at such a fence.

Bounces come in a variety of formats, either as a single bounce or incorporated into a more complex type of fence. Again, these can be practised at home before meeting them on the cross country course. They are not difficult in themselves but do require a balanced, steady approach with the horse off its forehand.

Most grids should incorporate a bounce so that the horse will learn the basic technique for jumping them early in its training. As it progresses, it will meet many bounce fences in competitions, so it should be confident enough to do a single and double bounce quite easily. Do not make the mistake of starting with jumps that are too high on a young horse. When practising at home, build up the height, making the first jump slightly lower than the second. Once your horse is jumping a good 91-cm (3-ft) bounce you can add a third element, making it a double bounce. The distances between them should be 3.6–4.5 m (12–15 ft) or four to five good walking strides.

RIGHT *Owen Moore and Blackberry Way demonstrate how spray can obliterate the horse's view, which can prove quite a problem if there is a jump out of the water. Slow the pace if this is likely to happen.*

BELOW *Gary Parsonage and Magic Rogue beautifully balanced as they jump down this drop at Blenheim Three-Day Event.*

ABOVE *Mary Thomson and King William in relaxed mood as they watch others do their dressage at Badminton in 1992.*

RIGHT *Concentration on the faces of both horse and rider while schooling before the dressage. Ian Stark and Glenburnie won the European Championships in Punchestown (Ireland) with a fine, all-round performance.*

RIGHT *New Zealand's Blyth Tait,
World Champion, takes Ra Ora
over the drop landing at Windsor
Three-Day Event. All riders like to
have younger horses to bring on
from the lower levels.*

BELOW *Lynne Bevan and Horton
Point jumping the steeplechase fences
in fine style at Badminton. Shorter
stirrups and a lighter rein are
required for this phase.*

Bruce Davidson has been at the top of American eventing for years and has won two World Championships. Here, he is jumping into Burghley's Trout Hatchery on Happy Talk.

LEFT *A delighted Ginny Leng holds the Mitsubishi Trophy after winning at Badminton 1993 with Welton Houdini.*

BELOW *Olympic Champions Matt Ryan and Kibah Tic Toc demonstrate supreme elegance and style across the arena in the dressage phase.*

LEFT *Sometimes horse and rider disagree as to how a fence should be negotiated!*

BELOW *Britain's Richard Walker and Jacana achieving a good clear round over the unusual, pastel-coloured show jumps at the Barcelona Olympics.*

ABOVE *Despite this spectacular entry into the water, both horse and rider emerged wet but unscathed.*

LEFT *A great jump by Nicholas Campbell and Nietsche over this imposing obstacle. Often called a 'rider frightener', this type of fence requires little effort from the horse but the depth of the ditch often causes quite a stir among the onlookers!*

LEFT *Sarah Norman does well to sit on China Faere as they enter the Trout Hatchery at Burghley. When a horse twists over a drop into water, the results can prove disastrous.*

BELOW *The distinctive style of Bruce Davidson is unmistakable as he clears this solid fence under the Copper Horse at Windsor.*

A bounce requires a positive, controlled approach, enabling the horse to remain balanced even though it has to take off again immediately after it has landed over the first element.

ABOVE AND OPPOSITE *This horse is learning the technique of jumping off a bank over a rail such as would be found at a Normandy bank. It is important not to land too steeply at such a fence but to jump out well, so that the horse does not peck on landing.*

For a very young horse, I usually make the first element a cross pole if the horse looks a little unsure about combinations in general. Once the technique has been mastered, however, most horses seem rather to enjoy demonstrating their athletic prowess.

Because there are so many different variations to bounces, keep your horse sharp and alert by jumping bounces throughout the year, sometimes building fences with a stride to a bounce or a bounce to a stride so that the horse learns to cope with such problems at any stage on the course.

Banks and steps are usually to be found in one form or another on every course. These may be just a jump up or a jump down, or may require an actual jump off the top of a fence, possibly over a rail or palisade, with a drop landing. Unless you have a step or bank at home, take the

ABOVE AND OPPOSITE *This rounded, flat bank requires a similar effort to the Normandy bank type but without having to jump up and over a rail off the bank.*

opportunity when out hacking to pop your horse over any safe ledge or to go down steep inclines as well as up them. Accustom the horse to going whenever it is asked. Keep your weight forward when going up hills or banks and in balance, either back or forwards, when coming down. Always give plenty of rein over a drop.

When schooling over proper banks or steps, start with the steps. It would be best to ask your young horse to pop off just one to start with. Some horses find the technique of jumping down very frightening, so if the horse can follow another the first time or two, this can be very helpful. Once the horse has been over one, any more are rarely a problem so long as you keep straight and remain positive. Teach the horse to trot towards steps to start with and then go from a balanced, steady canter. By going too fast you will increase the jar on landing.

A flat bank requires much the same technique when it comes to jumping off. Keep straight, keep your legs on so that you do not lose the forward impulsion and give well with your hands. A Normandy bank requires a jump over a fence on the bank with a drop off. This will most likely have one or two strides maximum on top but may also be a bounce on to the bank, then off again immediately. Ride positively to make the horse jump out well so that it does not pitch on landing.

When riding up steps or on to banks, be positive in your approach, keep your horse's head up and ride in a forward, bouncy canter. Really go forward with your horse as it springs upwards on to the steps or bank and then keep that momentum going forward without getting left behind and hindering the horse at any time.

On a series of steps up, the horse will tend to jump a little shorter on to each step because of the effort of going uphill. The rider must help to keep up the forward momentum by riding each step and maintaining the rhythm throughout. All too often you see a good positive approach to these fences, then, just when the horse needs most encouragement, the rider merely sits there so that, by the time the horse gets to the top of three or four steps, it is really struggling.

Water should present few problems if the horse has been ridden regularly through safe streams, puddles and over small fences over, into, before or after water. Confidence is everything with water and it is imperative that the horse never has an unnecessary fright at a fence into water. Always ensure that the bottom is safe and the water not too deep. The test for the horse is that it jumps into the water, not whether it is 15–46 cm (6–18 in) deep. The latter depth is too deep for the horse to land safely as it is the second stride in that tends to cause the drag that can make the horse stumble. The accepted maximum depth for the landing is 30 cm (12 in), so, in order to build up confidence, do not jump into anything with a greater depth than this.

Always start your water-jump training with simple, straightforward fences. With the young horse, it may be best to go into the water first and get its feet wet, then jump out. The next stage will be a jump in. Take it slowly in trot to start with so that the horse learns to pop in without too big a jump. This is a most important lesson to learn as you are much

A textbook example as dual Olympic champions Mark Todd and the diminutive Charisma sail into the water complex at the Seoul Olympics – balanced, confident and neat.

more likely to encounter problems if you have an exaggerated jump in with the risk of a peck or stumble on landing.

The horse must learn to be economical with its jump and it may take two or three sessions for it to relax enough to master this if it is the type that overjumps into water. If there is a jump out, it is vital that the horse focuses on this so that it makes a clean jump out and does not 'miss' by being overexuberant going into the water. So often the fence into the water is negotiated safely but it is on the exit that there is an upset, so make the horse concentrate throughout the combination.

Some water fences require the horse to jump a fence in the water. This is usually clearly visible to the horse as long as it does not create too much spray. Again, a steady approach is required until the horse is aware of what it is expected to do. A steady canter or strong trot is then the best gait in which to approach these.

Try to set as straight a route as possible through water. Turning is not easy and can tend to unbalance the horse, so do not turn too suddenly if you can avoid it. Always try to give your horse a good view of the obstacle before you arrive at it, if possible. In this way the horse has time to adjust to the situation and is not confronted with a sudden problem by being turned into it at the last moment. Build up confidence at each stage by making everything easy for the horse wherever you can. It will really pay off in the end.

Special obstacles There are several fences that have become features of eventing, including bullfinches, trakehners, coffins, tiger traps, etc, all of which require a slightly different technique in order to jump them. Although all fences need careful thought as to how to make the best approach and what is the best getaway, it is vital to assess every fence anew on the approach as so much may have happened since you actually walked the course. A fence may also look different with the crowds around it and after a few horses have been over it, possibly cutting up the ground.

Bullfinches can be rather imposing if they are high and thick, particularly to the young horse. After the horse has made a big leap over such a fence, when it is perhaps a bit overawed, the landing can be a bit

The downhill approach to Gatcombe's water complex requires balance and control but also enough impulsion to ensure that you get into the water. The fence going out is not easy as there is only half a stride of grass in front of it, which is a bit confusing for the horse.

exciting so the rider will need to be braced for whatever may materialize. The experienced horse should brush through without problems, depending on the thickness. However, do not underestimate these fences as they do often cause a big jump. Be prepared to sit tight over the bigger ones.

Because of its somewhat daunting appearance, the young horse may be totally thrown by such a fence if it has not encountered one in training. If you have a brush fence, stick some long, high twigs in this and jump your horse over it a few times before making it more imposing with thicker greenery or dense brush.

There are variations to the traditional type of bullfinch, such as a more definite firebeater design in which certain sections stick up quite high in the air, leaving narrow gaps through which to jump. Accuracy and boldness are necessary, and it is a good idea to tie a few bundles of twigs to a small fence to give the horse a bit of an idea about this type of fence early in its training.

Do not make the mistake of frightening the horse off altogether by making it too big or difficult at first. Just make it obvious to the horse that it must jump between narrow things sometimes. All it needs to learn is the technique of going straight and with confidence through such a fence.

Trakehners are often rather off-putting, especially if they have a wide and airy ditch underneath. However, they are often more worrying to the rider than the horse! They need strong riding, with the rider looking and riding forward rather than looking down into the ditch, which will inevitably result in the horse losing its forward momentum, so you must remain positive.

The single rail can be placed in the middle or more towards the take-off or landing, or it can lie diagonally across the ditch. If you can practise small ones to begin with, the larger ones will cause no problems.

Because they have a rather gappy appearance anyway, trakehners are rarely big. The thicker the pole or log, the more inviting they are. Sometimes they are set in a bit of a drop, making their approach more difficult and rather uninviting. Hold the horse together and ride on strongly.

Trakehners involve a single rail or log over a ditch. For the spooky horse, the ditch can pose a bit of a problem but with strong, positive riding this is usually overcome. Certainly, this combination have no worries.

Zig-zags are rather similar to some trakehners (especially if they have a ditch underneath), but they require a little more accuracy on the approach if the angles are narrow. They can look rather confusing from a distance but become more obvious as you get nearer. Because of the

Small zig-zags rarely cause a problem as long as the rider is positive. More acute ones, with longer poles, require a steady, but forward, approach without standing off too far.

optical illusion, which can occasionally confuse both rider and horse, these fences do need to be treated with a bit of respect. Once you have decided on the part to be jumped, ride straight and strongly over.

Shallow zig-zags can be jumped more or less anywhere as long as you make the decision positively as to where this is to be. For those fences that have very deep zig-zags using long poles, it is probably best to jump across one of the angles, choosing whichever looks the most inviting. It is not a good idea to jump the point going away from you in case the horse is encouraged to stand off from the diagonal poles coming out towards it. It could then risk landing on the back point, causing an injury. Occasionally, if the point facing towards you has been made particularly inviting, an accurate, confident jump is worth taking on but do not take risks unless you have much to gain and, with a zig-zag, there is so little time to be saved or wasted that it is worth getting your approach right from the onset.

Fences that require a jump through a **barn** or **overhang** occasionally cause serious problems for a horse that dislikes low things and have even been known to stop top-class horses on rare occasions. If they are very low, they can make the horse duck its head on take-off, which can be a little unnerving.

Start the young horse off with an easy fence with a 'lid' that is high enough not to interfere with the jump or worry the horse unduly. Very often horses tend to duck their heads as they go over the fence, which can result in them knocking the fence, so keep a good hold of the head. Once the horse has been over a few fences with a 'top', they rarely worry about them and few horses are perturbed by the more advanced type of 'hole' to be jumped through, which is altogether quite narrow and low.

Coffins come in a variety of styles, often being sited on totally flat ground and incorporating the classic rails to a ditch to rails out with, usually, one or two strides in and out. Traditionally, however, the ditch is in a hollow with the rails producing a downhill approach on the way in and an uphill one on the way out. Sometimes coffins have two ditches with a variety of striding through these, or you may come across 'half coffins', featuring a rail followed by a ditch or a ditch followed by a rail. All require a balanced, steady approach with plenty of impulsion and quite a degree of athletic ability to be able to negotiate all three parts from differently angled ground.

It is always worth spending some time, both with young horses and with more experienced ones, just reminding them of what is involved. I usually start my young horses off by popping backwards and forwards

over the ditch alone, to ensure that this holds no horrors for them, and then jump the ditch, followed by the rail out. I finish off by jumping all three elements as it should be done, hopefully finishing with the horse full of confidence as to how to tackle such an obstacle.

There is, of course, an endless range of new fences appearing annually, some of which cause surprise and, in some cases, trepidation as to how they should be jumped, but, generally, they will all turn out to be variations of one or more of those already mentioned.

OPPOSITE AND BELOW *Coffins vary in difficulty, depending on their location, but, in general, require a controlled approach with determined riding through each element. This rider is keeping up the momentum all the way through.*

5

FAST WORK, GROUND CONDITIONS AND THE WEATHER

FAST WORK

For a really successful partnership to continue to progress, it is essential to look critically at every aspect of your training. It is no good being good at one discipline but not at another, especially if you want to be a successful eventer, therefore each part of your work must be looked at to establish how and where things could be improved. Flat work always needs practice as few riders can ever really master the standard that is required to be at the top. Building and maintaining fitness and coping with the demands of this, along with jump training, involves much time and effort, and also careful planning to ensure that the horse receives all the training it requires but is not pushed too far either mentally or physically. It is quite easy to go over the top and do just that little bit too much, which can so easily undo all the good you have spent months in achieving.

Once your horse is going well on the flat and its training in general is up to standard, you must start thinking of getting it sharpened up for the final run-up to the event. Fast work requires that you achieve a gradual build-up, and this is the case whether you are doing interval training, the more traditional gradual increase in work or a combination of both.

Galloping should always be done on good ground and preferably uphill so that the front legs take the minimum strain. A carefully worked-out plan at the beginning of the season will enable you to build up to your season's competitions. Having decided on my goal for the season, I find it best to work backwards from there (including other competitions which count as fast work) to where I have planned my first serious bit of fast work. With most horses I start fast work 2–4 weeks before the first event, but this depends on the individual horse's condition and fitness.

There are several points to bear in mind when doing fast work and these are listed below:

1 always work on good ground;
2 keep the horse balanced between hand and leg at all times;
3 never overtax the horse but work within its fitness limits;
4 monitor its recovery rates to ensure that progress is being made;
5 remember that warming-up and cooling-off are as important as the gallop itself. Take time over this.

Choosing your galloping ground is as important as the work itself as it is essential to keep the horse sound and take no risks. Whether you use a large field, a straight track or do short, sharp spurts along different tracks through the countryside is relatively unimportant, but the ground you do it on is crucial, particularly when the weather has been very dry or very wet for some time.

Uneven ground can so easily give a tweak to a tendon or joint, as can hard or soft ground. Learn to be observant and watch where you are riding so that it becomes second nature to you to choose good going. Many highly successful eventers have trained in a fairly unexciting field or up a hill and have managed to adapt their work, either by cantering more often over the same ground or going faster over shorter distances and alternating this with longer distances at a slower speed.

It is possible to train the horse in many different ways as long as what you are doing is progressive. Some people have wonderful facilities but never seem to have fit horses! Gradually work up to the speed that you will be required to go at in competition, but not over the same distance to start with. It must be a gradual process.

Speed and Distances

Most people canter their horses every fourth to sixth day, depending on the type of horse. In all probability, the warmblood will require more fast work than the Thoroughbred. I generally find that my early canters are at a speed of around 350 mpm. After a few times at this speed, I will first increase the distance, then slowly increase the speed to 400 mpm. After a few canters at that speed and then an increase in the distance, the speed increases again, through 450 to 500 mpm and so on, depending on the standard of competition for which I am training.

For national competitions at one-day events in the UK, cross country speeds vary from 490 mpm at Pre-Novice or Training levels to 600 mpm for Advanced. In International three-day events the cross

ENDURANCE

Phase	1-Star (★)	2-Star (★★)	3-Star (★★★)	4-Star (★★★★)
A & C	220 mpm 40–55 min 8800–12100 m	220 mpm 50–65 min 11000–14300 m	220 mpm 60–75 min 13200–16500 m	220 mpm 70–85 min 15400–18700 m
B	640 mpm 3.5 min 2240m	660 mpm 3.5 or 4 min 2310 or 2640 m	690 mpm 4 or 4.5 min 2760 or 3105 m	690 mpm 4.5 or 5 min 3105 or 3450 m
Max Jumping Efforts	6–8	6–8	6–8	8–10
D	520 mpm 7.5–9.5 min 3900–4940 m	550 mpm 9–11 min 4950–6050 m (520 mpm for Juniors)	570 mpm 10–12 min 5700–6840 m (550 mpm for Young Riders)	570 mpm *CCI: 12–14 min 6840–7980 m **CCIO: 13–14 min 7410–7980 m
Max Jumping Efforts	30	35	40	45

JUMPING

	1-Star (★)	2-Star (★★)	3-Star (★★★)	4-Star (★★★★)
	350 mpm 102–120 sec 600–700 m	375 mpm 104–120 sec 650–750 m	400 mpm 105–120 sec 700–800 m	400 mpm 113–128 sec 750–850 m

*   Concours Complet International
**   Concours Complet International Officiel

Table of speeds, times, distances and jumping efforts for three-day events.

country and steeplechase speeds increase from one-star (★) level up to three-star (★★★) level. Four-star (★★★★) events have the same speeds as three-star level but involve longer endurance and more jumping effort.

Most people who have not competed much find it difficult to learn about speed and distance. Having found a good area to gallop on, you can measure out 1,000, 1,500 or even 2,000-m stretches. Alternatively, you can ask someone to drive a car at the correct speed along a *quiet* road while you canter in the field on the other side of the hedge.

This will help you to work out your exact speed in metres per minute, to help you to gauge your times and distances. You can then work out how fast you need to go over various different distances by marking off the distances you want to practise and then using a watch to work out how long it should take you to canter each distance at each speed. This will take time but if you stick to one speed until you get the feel of that pace, you will soon discover that you can do it without using your watch.

It is very difficult to get your speeds right on a cross country course as so many factors will affect how fast you can actually go. By their very nature, the jumps themselves may slow you down, particularly the combination fences and water jumps, whereas a single fence on flat ground may be quicker as you will be missing out a couple of strides while in the air.

Ground conditions will also make a big difference to your speed, and if the terrain is undulating and hilly or runs through wooded areas, this will slow your speed down considerably. On very hard ground, the horse will tend to shorten its stride because of the jarring, while in deep going it will be slow because its feet are sinking into the ground further, which restricts the forward momentum. Some horses have naturally short strides, while others take great, long sweeping ones, so you will need to be able to feel the difference with each horse if you have more than one.

Rhythm is essential if you are to take as little out of your horse as possible. A free-flowing round will tire the horse far less than one in which it is endlessly being pulled back or pushed forward. It is much easier to evaluate your speed if the horse is going consistently in a steady rhythm.

Some courses are easy to ride within the time but others are very difficult so the more you keep flowing steadily on, the easier it will be to achieve a good time. It is during the approach and landing over a fence that time is lost unless the rider works to eliminate this. If you can always take the quickest route through a fence, with the least amount of time spent actually negotiating the obstacle, and then always take the most direct route towards the next fence, you will at least have ensured that no unnecessary time has been wasted.

FURTHER FITNESS WORK

For the eventer, fitness is an ongoing process, especially if you are aiming for a three-day or higher standard of event later in the season. It is the horse's stamina that requires working on, so that the horse will find it easy to compete without strain. The tendons and ligaments must be kept in good condition so that the horse is less likely to suffer injury. Normal work should involve as much of the same type of work that will be expected in competition as possible.

General fitness work can be slotted into the programme two or three times a week and should involve hacking out over natural countryside, through fields, along tracks and going up and down hills at a steady trot with the horse working nicely up to the bit. Walk on a long rein every ten minutes or so, then continue on your ride. If preparing for a three-day event, your preparatory work for the roads and tracks phase needs to be gradual. Your hacks out may start at about three-quarters of an hour to begin with but, after about six weeks, you need to be doing at least one and a half hours once or twice a week, keeping going in trot and canter most of the time.

A competiton or gallop can be considered a serious workout, so if you were doing either of these then one serious hack would be ample for that week. Once the horse has started to compete, it is unlikely that it will need more than one good hack or gallop a week anyway as long as you keep it working on the flat or give it a jump in between.

Every horse must be treated as an individual in everything that you do with it and a programme should be worked out to ensure that the horse has done everything you feel it needs to do and is confident about it before actually competing.

GROUND CONDITIONS

The ground can play a quite significant part in how well your horse performs. Some horses feel confident in all going and will carry on regardless of whether the ground is hard or soft, slippery or deep. Others, however, are not so happy and can quickly lose confidence in adverse conditions. This type of horse requires careful handling,

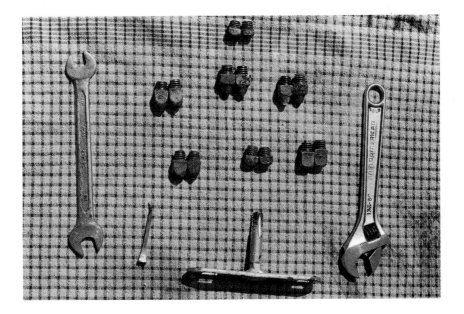

There are numerous different designs of stud, some of which are shown here. Their use can be invaluable, especially with young and inexperienced horses, which quickly lose confidence if they start to slide about.

especially in the early stages before it has done enough to build up its ability and confidence over a variety of fences and courses.

With such horses, the judicious use of studs can be beneficial and can make all the difference as to how the horse jumps. I tend to use small, sharp, road studs in hard ground, longish ones in deep going and very large ones in greasy going. If the ground is really good, I seldom use studs at all on experienced horses but would always use hind ones on younger horses. Make sure you school your horse with studs in if the ground is at all unsatisfactory, so that the horse feels safe. This is important in building up confidence. The horse should be regularly schooled over small fences in less than perfect going but should never be allowed to lose confidence by being too ambitious. When you actually compete, take care not to overface the horse if the ground is bad, especially if you go late in the day and the approaches to the fences have become very cut up. With a young horse, I would actually withdraw if I was unhappy but with an older one you might just as well try to snap up some prizes as several others might not be feeling so brave!

When competing in deep ground, it is important to remember how much bigger the fences will become when the horse has sunk about 7 cm

(½ in) into the mud, so more determined riding will be required and distances will often feel long if the horse is finding the ground sticky. Usually, stronger riding will make up for the deep going. If the horse is tending to back off, be prepared to ride it strongly forward and keep the momentum going as nothing is more demoralizing for a horse than to struggle over big fences with no help from on top.

Hard, slippery going can be equally off-putting for the horse and may affect an older horse even more than a youngster, as the older horse will be more wary of the jarring effect. Ideally, do not ride if the ground is rock-hard, but this is not always practical if qualifications etc are being sought. The horse will probably shorten its stride as it will not want to be airborne a moment longer than necessary. You will need to be prepared to ride on if this happens, especially at combinations.

Very greasy conditions can be quite nerve-wracking as then horses tend to slip around all over the place, but, with a bit of common sense, it is often possible to take a fresh line just to the right or left of centre and get on some fresh ground. This is not so easy when riding a corner, however, as, on most occasions, you will have to ride where everyone else has jumped or take the longer route if the ground in front of the fence really is very poached.

Riding on sandy going may be fairly non-slip but it can also ride very 'dead' and some horses do not like this too much, shortening their stride and often changing legs frequently.

Ground conditions can have an amazing effect on how well a horse copes with the course. If the ground is a bit on the firm side, the horse will generally fly round with relative ease, whether it is a bit too hard for its liking or not. In really soft, holding ground, it may become very tired indeed and not finish the course in anything like the state of fitness that you were expecting after the amount of work you have done in training.

Do not despair if this happens. It is very tiring for anyone, horse or person, to run in ground that is deep. Check your horse's recovery rate and assess the course. Watch other horses finishing, see if and how much they vary from yours and ask yourself a few searching questions. Did you go too fast for the state of the ground; was the horse ready to compete in the first place; had you taken away its feed and hay early enough in advance; is it unwell?

Such questions require thorough investigation before you can be satisfied that your horse was, in fact, ready for the conditions and the work being asked of it. If you are not satisfied, have the horse checked out thoroughly in case it has a virus or is suffering from any other malady that could affect its performance in this way.

HEAT AND HUMIDITY

Another factor that can seriously affect how well the horse will go is the weather. Hot and humid conditions can be very dehydrating and will certainly make a big difference to the performance of the horse. The fitter the horse, the better it will be able to cope with such conditions but several other factors will also affect the degree to which it can tolerate heat and/or humidity. Never underestimate the effect that weather conditions can have on your horse's performance.

The breeding of the horse will play a significant role. Thoroughbreds or Thoroughbred types generally cope better in hot and humid conditions. A leaner horse will be able to cool itself much more effectively than a fat one, through sweating, nature's most effective cooling mechanism. The fat horse has better insulation, which makes heat loss more difficult. It will have to use its lungs more and pant to help to increase heat loss in extreme conditions. This may brings its respiratory and pulse rate up to approximately 200 beats per minute.

The speed at which the horse is expected to work will have a great effect on how well it is able to perform in hot or humid conditions, so that asking the horse to work at fast speeds may seriously detract from its ability to finish the competition. The rider will need to draw on all their knowledge and experience to be able to ride the horse within its capability in such conditions, yet go well enough to be in a good position at the end.

The action of the horse will also affect how it performs. A horse with flowing paces will take less out of itself than a more exaggerated mover who puts more effort into each stride.

The horse must be in peak physical condition before being subjected to competitive work in hot and humid conditions. It must have been regularly wormed, had its teeth checked, be receiving the right food for what it is doing and have been prepared carefully for the competition in every way.

Preventing Heatstroke and Dehydration

In extreme conditions, the horse's natural methods of cooling itself will be put under great stress. If this becomes too great, the horse's own system may prove inadequate, allowing the body temperature to rise too high. The horse loses heat through its skin, by sweating and evaporation, and through its lungs by breathing out warmer air than it is taking in. It will only actually pant when sweating becomes inadequate to cool it

down sufficiently and this is an indication that the horse is becoming severely stressed.

If you are concerned about dehydration, try the pinch test, by taking hold of a fold of skin, usually on the lower neck. If this does not return to normal when released, but remains sticking up, this indicates dehydration. The horse loses large amounts of electrolytes through sweat and unless these are maintained in the correct balance, normal metabolism will be affected. As the horse can lose up to 15 litres (3 gal) of sweat an hour in extreme conditions, it is important to prevent dehydration by ensuring that the horse is offered frequent small drinks of both fresh, not too cold, water and also water containing electrolytes so that lost electrolytes are quickly replaced. The horse is not very efficient at maintaining the correct balance of its body salts in hot conditions and therefore quick action may be needed.

OPPOSITE AND BELOW *At the higher levels, eventing is a strenuous sport, requiring quality horses which are well trained and fit for the job. Fences such as this imposing step combination require a lot of energy and athletic ability.*

The effect of dehydration on the horse causes its blood supply to become thicker and more concentrated. The oxygen-carrying capability of the blood then becomes less effective and the energy stored in the muscles begins to break down through anaerobic respiration. This releases lactic acid into the muscles, which may damage the muscle fibres and also cause azoturia or tying up.

If the horse's cooling mechanism through sweating becomes ineffective, its temperature rises above 40.5°C (105°F) and the horse starts to pant, or if its respiratory rate begins to exceed the pulse rate, you must call the vet immediately before the situation gets out of hand. Any horse with a temperature that is higher than this should not be allowed to continue to work. The horse may also display a quivering of the muscles known as a diaphragmatic flutter or 'the thumps'. If this happens urgent veterinary care is vital.

The care of the horse in hot conditions can make an enormous difference to how it copes. One of the classic ways for a horse to become dehydrated is to leave it standing in a hot lorry or trailer for several hours. Lack of water is another cause, so ensure that this is freely available up to an hour before competing. The horse will be unlikely to drink excessively anyway if water is always available. Make sure the horse has an empty stomach before work, so that its system is not working on the digestion of food when the horse should be competing.

Washing down, for example during the ten-minute halt after the steeplechase, and second roads and tracks phase of a three-day event, should involve a thorough soaking with cool water, followed by a period of cooling before scraping away excess water and allowing for another washdown. Iced water can be used against the large surface veins, arteries, throat and head to assist in cooling. Care must be taken when using iced water in very hot weather, however, as it can cause stiffness and tightening of the long muscles and will tend to constrict the blood vessels of the skin, thus preventing heat from being dispersed so effectively. The situation must be studied each time with every horse to assess how hot it is and which priority should come first. A clean sponge of cold water can be squeezed into its mouth to refresh it but no more water should be offered at this stage if the horse is about to set off across country.

The type of tack you use can also play a part as the larger the area this covers, the hotter the horse is likely to get, so avoid large saddle pads or synthetic materials which do not allow the skin to breathe so readily. The smaller the area that is covered, the larger the area that is available for natural evaporation and cooling.

After the endurance phase, it is just as important to cool the horse well, using the same principles. Washdown, cool, scrape, washdown, cool, scrape, etc, until the horse is relaxed and refreshed. Walking it quietly until its pulse and respiration rates are virtually back to normal is essential to ensure that all the waste products that have built up in the muscles during anaerobic exertion have dispersed. Keep the horse cool and offer it frequent drinks of up to half a bucket of cool water until it is satisfied. The tired horse may be reluctant to start drinking, so keep on offering water even if it looks uninterested to begin with.

TIPS FOR SUCCESS

Weather conditions can have a considerable impact on the horse during exertion. Cool conditions are ideal for endurance events but they can become a nightmare when it is hot and/or humid. In such conditions, the way the rider nurses the horse through will considerably assist or hinder its recovery rates throughout the day.

Bright sunshine, hot and humid conditions or very sticky ground test the horse's stamina to the utmost. The way the jockey rides in such conditions can have an enormous bearing on the final outcome.

A minimum weight of 75 kg (165 lb) has to be carried in three-day events and Advanced classes. If a lot of weight needs to be carried, make sure it is evenly distributed on either side. This rider appears to be carrying a lot behind the saddle. Try to keep the weight further forward, nearer the horse's centre of gravity.

Picking the best ground, riding in an even rhythm, rising up out of the saddle and staying off the horse's back will all help considerably towards making the horse's task easier. The even distribution of any weights carried, the comfort of the tack worn, the weight of the horse's shoes and non-absorbency of boots and bandages will all add to, or detract from, a successful outcome.

The even distribution of weights is essential but care must also be taken to ensure that the weight cloth is not pressing down on the withers. If you are carrying large amounts of lead, this could seriously hinder the horse and can result in loss of performance because of the pressure on this sensitive area. Pull the weight cloth and numnah well up into the front arch of the saddle and then strap the weight cloth to this to help to keep the weight off the horse's back.

The weight factor is not considered nearly enough by three-day event riders, in my opinion. I am always horrified to see so many horses carrying such heavy shoes. When you think that these have to be picked up by the horse with every stride it takes, you will realize that this soon turns into tonnes. Add to this any extra weight you may be carrying yourself and you will begin to realize how much we take for granted from our four-footed friends.

Correct shoeing is something that can be discussed with your farrier. Your horse needs shoes that are light enough not to hinder it unduly in any way, while being robust enough to do the job in the conditions likely to be met. Always take a spare set with you to competitions and also ensure that your horse has been recently shod before competing. It is a bit risky to shoe immediately prior to competing in case the horse feels a bit sore in any way as then there will not be time to put it right. However, every horse is different and some

Many a horse has gone lame through incorrect or too infrequent shoeing. The competition horse is likely to need shoeing at least every three to four weeks. Always carry a spare set with you in case you lose one on the day.

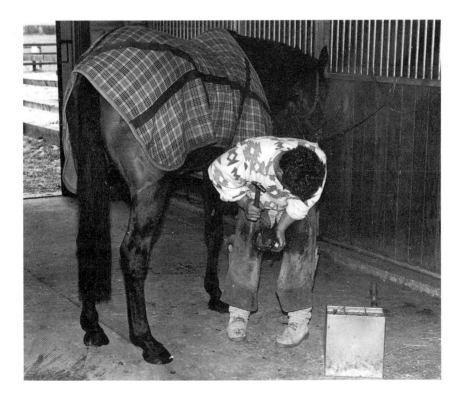

ABOVE AND OPPOSITE *It is essential for the successful cross country rider to know how to bridge the reins – invaluable if you tend to get too far forward on landing on a bold horse or over drop fences. Bridge the reins and wedge your hands into the horse's neck for security.*

are best shod close to an event, especially if they tend to be heavy on shoes. I usually get mine shod about one week to ten days before a major event, to give the shoes time to settle.

Staying in the shade, offering regular drinks and keeping your horse cool are all factors that will help it to cope in hot conditions. When the horse starts to travel or if it becomes very hot in training, a small daily supplement of electrolytes can be helpful in maintaining hydration. However, beware of upsetting the natural balance of salts by giving too many electrolytes too soon or if conditions do not warrant it, as you could cause an imbalance that is potentially dangerous. Supplement with electrolytes only as demand dictates, but give them whenever you are likely to encounter hot or humid conditions.

In hot weather, ensure that the horse has plenty to drink and offer small drinks frequently up to half an hour before competing. Remember also that nature's way of cooling the horse is through sweat and evaporation, so the larger the area available to do this, the more effective it will be. The lighter and more naturally absorbent your equipment is, the better. Cotton numnahs covering as small an area as possible should be the rule. Large square pads will increase the heavily sweating area and so add to dehydration.

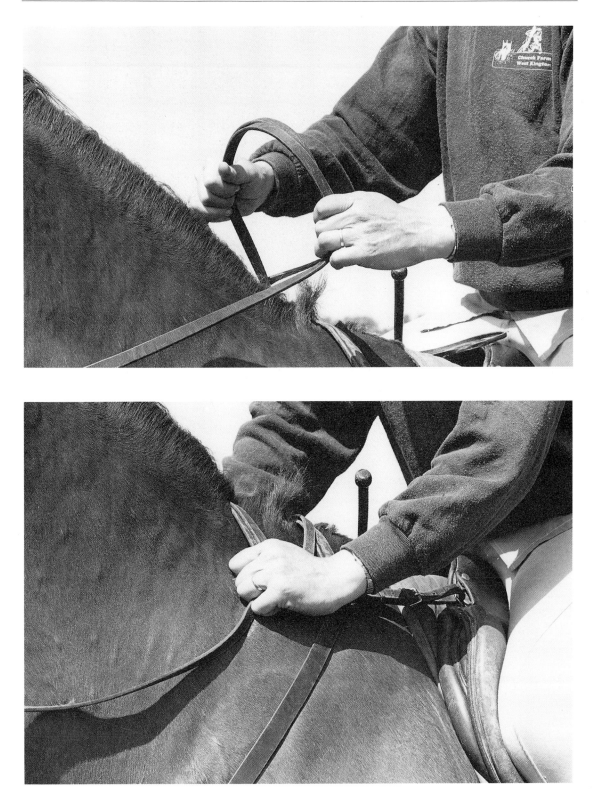

Make sure your tack is always maintained in good condition and is safe and comfortable. Very narrow breastplates or girths can cut into a sensitive horse's skin and tight, narrow girths have caused haematomas. Consider whether wider girths would be more comfortable if your horse is prone to rubs or swellings. Ensure that all tack is kept soft and supple and fits the horse well. Bridles can be uncomfortable if browbands pinch behind the ears or throatlashes are too tight.

Tips on how to 'bridge your reins' are vital for steeplechasing and cross country riding, and the ability to extend your legs forwards on landing is always invaluable. Don't just assume these things will come to you. Get advice from an expert and make sure you do them properly.

Safe tack is essential to safe riding. This dramatic shot of Ian Stark and Glenburnie, European Champions in 1991, clearly demonstrates the strain that is put on the tack at certain fences.

6

COMPETING AT EVENTS

After the endless training that goes into preparing the Advanced cross country horse, it comes as a welcome relief when you actually arrive at the competition. Every horse is different and each will require a different amount of time to reach the top levels. Some will never get there, through lack of soundness or physical or mental ability. Others are simply not cut out for the sport and, sadly, many are ruined along the way by being rushed before they are ready to cope with the demands made on them.

ONE-DAY EVENTS

One-day events provide the training ground for those who ultimately want to compete in a three-day event. A one-day event consists of dressage, show jumping and a cross country course. In most cases these are all carried out on one day, although some competitors may be asked to perform the dressage on the previous day if there are too many entries.

Riders compete at the various levels of a one-day event in order to gain qualifications and to give their horses the experience needed to compete in three-day events. Because the cross country courses are relatively short it is possible for horses to compete in several one-day events throughout the year, whereas it is generally accepted that two three-day events in one year are sufficient because of the amount of work and training necessary to achieve adequate fitness.

At one-day events in Britain the dressage section is generally followed by the show jumping phase, with the cross country last. Occasionally, however, for special classes or in one-day championships the show jumping is carried out after the cross country to give competitors more of an idea of how the horse feels after the exertions of the cross country.

In the United States and in many other countries it is the norm for the show jumping to follow the cross country phase. There is no doubt that it is much more difficult to achieve a clear round in the show jumping after the horse has been galloping and has, therefore, jumped flatter over the fences that when it is more obedient and fresh to the rider's demands.

TWO-DAY EVENTS

Two-day events provide a useful stepping stone from one-day to three-day events and are particularly useful for giving the less experienced rider an insight into what is necessary when tackling the speed and endurance phases, known as Phases A to D.

Generally, the dressage and show jumping are run on the first day and the speed and endurance phases on the second day. The speed and endurance phases consist of the first roads and tracks (Phase A), which acts as a warm-up. The steeplechase over between four and ten fences (Phase B) demonstrates the horse's ability to jump at speed. The second roads and tracks (Phase C) is the cooling-off period. This is followed by a compulsory ten minute break when an inspection panel looks over the horses and passes them fit to continue. Phase D – the cross country – follows. This is when horse and rider shown their ability and training over various cross country obstacles. The competitor with the least penalties is the winner.

THREE-DAY EVENTS

Three-day events are now classified, according to their standard, by a 'star' system. One star indicates a Novice standard course, two Intermediate standard, three Advanced and four Championship level, which includes Britain's Badminton and Burghley three-day events. All of these competitions are run under Federation Equestre Internationale (FEI) rules for three-day events. Special dressage tests are used for each standard, and set speeds and distances, as well as fence heights, are specified for each level. (See the charts on pp.158–9.)

RIDING THE DRESSAGE TEST AT A COMPETITION

The art of riding a good test in front of judges is not easily mastered, except by those at the very top, who somehow make it look easy! It is most important to forget any inhibitions or nervousness you may feel, and go out to present your horse and yourself in the best possible light during the few minutes you are in front of the judges.

They are looking for obedience, suppleness, rhythm and evidence of correct training during the set movements of the test. It must look easy and flowing, be a pleasure to watch and get good marks!

Presentation is everything. First and foremost, sit up and look the part, with your horse going forward in a good outline and held between your hand and leg. Everything about your test must show forward movement without restriction. All movements must be ridden accurately and show the differences in pace required.

Throughout the test, be positive in your riding and do not make the mistake of 'sitting pretty' and showing nothing to the judges. They can only assess what they see happening in front of them – so really 'go for it' to get the good start so vital for success.

RIDING THE ROADS AND TRACKS (PHASES A AND C)

This is just as important as the steeplechase and cross country phases of a three-day event. It is during Phases A and C that so much preparation is done for the next phase and how this is done will affect the horse's performance during the rest of the competition.

Phase A is the warm-up phase. Its object is to loosen and supple the horse and prepare it for the steeplechase. I see little point in doing anything more serious than five to ten minutes' walking prior to setting off on this phase. Once I have weighed out for the two- or three-day event at which I am riding, I generally get on about five minutes before my official start time. Keep the horse moving and calm because, inevitably, this is quite a tense moment for you, the horse and, particularly, your helpers, who have such a nerve-wracking time until it is all safely over!

Set off quietly from the start box. This is not a fast phase so there is little point in taking more out of the horse than necessary. Establish a good rhythm at the horse's most relaxed gait – either a steady trot or a slow, lolloping canter.

If trotting, remember to rise and sit as lightly as possible on the horse's back and to change diagonals frequently so that the horse does not get a stiff back from constantly pushing your weight up with every stride on the same diagonal. Very often, I come up off the horse's back for a couple of hundred metres or so and then let it swing along underneath me. Rise gently up and down in the saddle; do not be one of those riders who bang down heavily with every stride.

Phases A and C are carried out at a speed of 220 mpm which is equivalent to a steady trot or slow canter for most horses. If you consider four minutes per kilometre as your basic guide, you will be about right. Obviously, some horses move quicker than others and some ground conditions will be better than others on these phases. You will ride rather quicker on good grass going than trotting up or down a steep track through woods or whatever. It may, therefore, work out that 1 km on good ground will take three minutes and 1 km on steep going will take five minutes. You must adapt the pace to suit your horse and the ground conditions.

Most people like to include a short, sharp gallop in Phase A, at between 550 and 600 mpm, to ensure that the horse is fully warmed up. This is generally not more than about 400–600 m (440–660 yd) long but should be carried out on a good piece of ground, ideally up a slight hill. Although this gallop is not essential, in higher-standard events it is a good idea to move your horse on at some stage to get the adrenalin flowing before it starts Phase B, the steeplechase.

There will be some places where you will need to go a little slower and some where less time is needed but try to stick to an average of four minutes. You should then find that you are left with enough time to finish Phase A, and allow between one and two minutes to check girths and shorten stirrups ready for Phase B, the steeplechase. Keep the horse walking and do not go into the start box too early, although it will prove very costly if you are not in before the starter says 'go', so time yourself to walk calmly in a circle and be ready for the off when the starter begins the countdown of 'five, four, three, two, one, go'.

After the steeplechase, you will go straight on to Phase C, so pull the horse up gradually, let it slow down to a walk and ride on a loose rein for a few minutes while you assess how the horse feels and how long you can afford to stay in walk. I normally like to pass the first kilometre on Phase C five minutes after finishing Phase B. If you get too far behind, you will find that you are always struggling to catch up and are never able to give the horse enough time to recover, which is the whole point of Phase C.

The first roads and tracks phase (A) acts as a warm-up before the steeplechase phase (B), and then the second roads and tracks phase (C) gives the horse time to recover from the steeplechase, before going on to tackle the cross country phase (D). Be sensitive to your horse's needs and keep up to time. This rider is checking his watch and has his times taped to his arm for reference.

The longer this phase is, the more time the horse has to recover from the exertion and speed of the previous phase. At Novice two- or three-day events, this phase tends to be on the short side, which is not advantageous to the horse. In Advanced events, Phase C is likely to be somewhere between 9 and 12 km (5½–7½ miles), which works out at around 40–50 minutes, and this gives the horse ample time to recover from the steeplechase. This means that it is likely to arrive back in the box afterwards in a better state, having had more time for its breathing to return to normal and to cool down properly under normal conditions. Anything under 5 km (3 miles) barely allows the horse enough time, even although it will have been a short steeplechase if Phase C is only around that distance.

Stick to the four minute per kilometre guide so that you do not fall behind, but slow up on the last couple of kilometres so that the horse is

Protecting both horse and rider makes sense when riding across country. Check the competition rules to ensure that your hat and body protector conform to requirements, and check that all other equipment is safe and appropriate for the conditions.

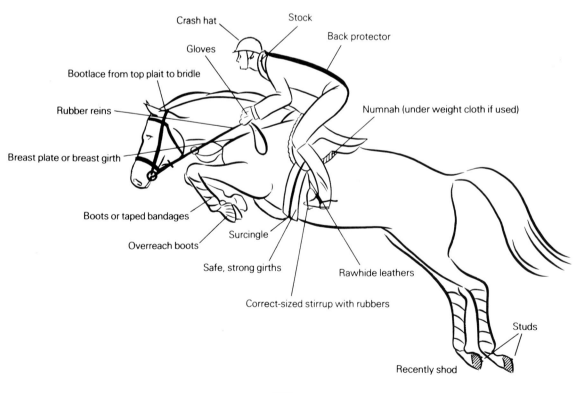

relaxed and calm as it comes in from Phase C, when it will be seen by the inspection panel. Be guided by their advice and then keep the horse moving quietly after a good washdown if this is indicated. I always try to get into the ten-minute box a couple of minutes before my official time, to allow the horse twelve minutes at this stage. Because the allowed time on Phases A and C is a little over four minutes per kilometre, your times will automatically allow for this with the longer Phase C that is met in three- and four-star events.

The care it receives in the ten-minute box plays a major role in how the horse will cope with the cross country phase, which will be discussed later in the chapter. In all phases the rider must try to take as little out of the horse as possible. Such things as rhythm, straightness in the saddle, calmness, choosing the best ground and the quickest route, as well as choice of tack, protective leg care and shoeing will all affect the performance. The rider therefore requires a sound knowledge of all these things in order to succeed and reach the top.

The Start Box

The start box can be quite an exciting area if a little quiet planning has not been done beforehand. Inevitably, there are a tense few moments just prior to setting off round either the steeplechase or cross country course, but your attitude at this point can help to keep the horse calm.

The most important thing to remember is to allow your horse to walk forwards. Any restriction at this time could easily result in a rear or worse, so try not to enter the start box a moment before it is necessary unless you need to do this early because the horse can be difficult to get in. Otherwise, just circle quietly with a loose and relaxed rein.

Some horses will gaze in the opposite direction quite quietly but behave like demons if turned to look towards the first fence. Some will refuse to go into the box at all and you may need a helper to lead it in quietly, taking care not to pull at its mouth in the process.

Timing is all-important around the start box. Make sure you are ready when called by the starter and avoid last-minute panics and a lot of dashing about if possible. Pre-plan who is doing what and when, and this will make a huge difference to the atmosphere around the horse. Talk through your procedure with your helpers prior to the actual start, so that everyone knows what to do. This should include who washes down, scrapes, puts on grease, if used, and gives you a leg up, as well as knowing who is going to tell you when you need to be at the start box for the count down.

RIDING THE STEEPLECHASE COURSE

The steeplechase phase inevitably contributes towards the way the horse goes on the cross country course. It gets the horse going, sharpens it up and generally sets the scene for what is to come. The higher speeds used for the steeplechase encourage the horse to fly through the top of its fences rather than bascule over them, wasting valuable seconds. For the cross country phase, the horse must readjust to being relatively alert and jump more cleanly over the obstacles.

Steeplechase practice is wise before your first three-day event, so that you are sure your horse can lengthen and stretch over these fences at a faster pace. Jumping beside another horse for a couple of schooling sessions gives encouragement to the careful jumper which wastes time by backing off its fences.

It is definitely to your advantage if you can shorten your stirrups to give you a little more leverage and a safer position over the fences. You will never see a steeplechase jockey riding long in a race. Ride well forwards and get the horse into a steady rhythm so that it will meet the fences on a good stride. Pulling or pushing the horse into the fences will upset this rhythm and take so much more out of it, as well as making it difficult to find a good take-off point.

Timing is vital on the steeplechase if you are not to incur heavy penalties for being outside the optimum time for your standard of event. Having had a few practices at home or on some gallops, your feel for this will be much easier if you have felt the speed at which you should be riding. The secret is to get out of the start box immediately the starter indicates 'go' so that you can quickly establish your rhythm and a good length of stride.

If the steeplechase consists of two circuits, starting and finishing in the same spot, it is easy to gauge your speed by looking at your stop watch as you come towards the end of the first circuit. Experienced riders should be able to assess their speed just through 'feel'. Generally, you will take around five to eight seconds longer on the first circuit than on the second because of the standing start and the time taken to establish your rhythm.

For the figure-of-eight type of course or those that are not uniform, it is more difficult to determine your speed if you do not know where the halfway point is and if everything looks different around the course. However, rhythm and balance are just as important as speed, so establish both as soon as possible and then it will be easier to decide if your speed is right.

Courses that are all on one rein can affect the way the horse pulls up afterwards. If it has been pounding round on the same leg for between three to five minutes, it is likely that it will feel leg weary on that leg unless it has changed legs somewhere on the way round. Do not be too surprised if the horse feels very unlevel for a hundred metres or so after you pull it up. Pull up steadily and keep the horse balanced and well held together so that it is less likely to trip or overextend on pulling up. Allow the horse a little trotting time to unwind before pulling up and then let it walk for a couple of minutes before continuing on your way round the roads and tracks.

The position of the rider during the steeplechase is well forward but safely braced over the knees in a secure galloping position. The hands must keep the horse steady in a good, even rhythm, and the rider must feel able to sit up safely and balance should the horse peck on landing.

Jumping fences at steeplechase speed requires a good sense of timing and consistent riding, all of which comes with experience. If you can get some help and advice from a jockey or trainer on how to ride over fences, this will prove invaluable. They are the real experts and can give you so much useful information.

THE CROSS COUNTRY PHASE (PHASE D)

The Aim of the Course Designer

The course designer's task is an unenviable one but undoubtedly counts as the most important job in the running of a horse trials. The aim is generally to set a course that will test the horse fairly, according to the standard of course, and make the rider think hard enough to sort out the good from the rest. To achieve this, the designer sites fences in such a way that each fence requires some thought and preparation without upsetting the horse's rhythm and flow round the course.

OPPOSITE AND BELOW *This trakehner-type fence looks more imposing to the rider, who knows the depth of the ditch, than to the horse, which will hardly see it anyway.*

ABOVE AND OPPOSITE *Corners require great accuracy and impulsion. These lovely pictures show horse and rider in complete harmony throughout and demonstrate how this type of fence should be jumped.*

There will be a straightforward start to encourage the horse to go forward and establish a rhythm before encountering any serious questions. These are generally more likely to be found towards the middle of the course. Every course builder has their own methods of testing horses and riders, and most are known for the type of course they build. Some favour uprights, others spreads with obvious groundlines, some use very big timber, others prefer a more subtle approach, some prefer bounces and arrowheads, while others go for corners every time, some will build smaller-looking fences that require more accurate riding from the rider, while others build big and technical fences or big and straightforward ones. It is always worth trying to analyse what the course designer is

aiming to achieve from the course and then set about riding it in accordance. If the designer wishes the course to be attacked boldly, you are not going to find it too easy if you amble up to the fences in a half-hearted manner. These will not be the sort of fences that the horse will find easy without positive help from its rider.

These charts show the differences in times and speeds used at three different three-day events at two-, three- and four-star levels. The higher speeds tend to take most out of the horse, so fitness and proper preparation are vital.

★★ 2-STAR THREE-DAY EVENT

Phase	Nature	Distance Metres	Speed Metres per min	Optimum time Min Sec
A	Roads & Tracks	3630	220	16 30
B	Steeplechase	2640	660	4 00
C	Roads & Tracks	7810	220	35 30
D	Cross Country	5020	550	9 08

★★★ 3-STAR THREE-DAY EVENT

Phase	Nature	Distance Metres	Speed Metres per min	Optimum time Min Sec
A	Roads & Tracks	4400	220	20 00
B	Steeplechase	2760	690	4 00
C	Roads & Tracks	8800	220	40 00
	Vet Inspection	–	–	10 00
D	Cross Country	5700	570	10 00

★★★★ 4-STAR THREE-DAY EVENT

Phase		Distance	Speed	Optimum time
	Nature	Metres	Metres per min	Min Sec
A	Roads & Tracks	6380	220	29 00
B	Steeplechase	3105	690	4 30
C	Roads & Tracks	9130	220	41 30
	Vet Inspection	—	—	10 00
D	Cross Country	6840	570	12 00

Assessing the Cross Country Course

Riding the cross country course itself is, without doubt, the most exhilarating and enjoyable aspect of our sport. The way this is carried out, planning beforehand and an ability to adapt to each situation as it arises will all contribute to the day's success or failure. It is up to the rider to concentrate their mind on the task ahead and give it their full and undivided attention.

Having walked the course carefully and seen where the problems are, you will have assessed how these are likely to affect your horse. You must then decide where you are going to jump each fence and whether you are simply out for a confidence-giving round, taking each fence straight, to give your horse the best possible chance. On the other hand, you may be going out to win, which requires taking quicker routes and going faster. Or you may be aiming just for a good ride and a clear round, without any further aspirations.

Your attitude will definitely affect how your horse reacts, and it is important to be well motivated and positive as you set off. How you jump the first few fences is likely to affect the rest of your round. A good start usually results in a confident performance. A horse that does not start well can take a long time to get going and settle into a rhythm. Some lose confidence altogether when things do not go well at the beginning. It is up to the rider to dictate how they intend their day to go so that both they and the horse start the course with a positive mental attitude.

The main problems on a cross country course usually involve combination or water fences. These two fences at Badminton include a bounce into water followed by a step up to an arrowhead out.

A fence such as this has several options. The rider must carefully assess which route would be best for the horse at that stage of the course rather than simply attempting the quickest route.

RIDING THE FENCES ON THE DAY

The weather, the ground and the speed and angle of approach can make all the difference as to how the fences jump. Always consider how these aspects might affect your round and take appropriate precautions when you ride.

The first fence should be a straightforward start to your round but you must treat it as the most importance fence of the day. Make sure the horse is concentrating and is focusing on the jump as you approach, not looking around it. The second, and sometimes the third, fences are normally fairly straightforward as well, depending on the standard, of course. Use these to build up confidence and settle your horse into that all-important rhythm.

Generally, from the third fence onwards, you will begin to encounter the first of the various problems likely to be met on the more advanced courses. When walking the course, think how they relate to the rest of the course. A good ride over an early corner, for example, may set you up for a more tricky one later on. If the more difficult corner comes early in the course, however, and you are aiming for a qualification, you might be wise to consider the bounce option, or whatever, at this early fence. Once you have got your horse settled and going as you want it to, you will feel more certain that you can jump the later fence accurately and clear.

Combinations

The combination fences on the course are often the most influential, requiring accuracy and commitment. Every fence is unique to that course on that day as so much can affect how it jumps in that particular competition. The ground, the light, your horse's experience, the condition of the take-off and landing, and the difficulty of the fences before the combination will all affect the way the fence is jumped.

It is very important to study the fence from every angle, especially if it is new to that course, so that you can assess every option thoroughly. Pace out the different options and work out which one would suit your horse best, taking into account its particular length of stride and ability. Do not forget to take note of a long galloping stretch before the combination, which will have given your horse a chance to really lengthen its stride. If the striding is short, you will now need to bring the horse back enough to cope with the combination.

A fence that incorporates a bounce will require strong rebalancing of the horse in order to bring its hocks far enough underneath it for it to find this easy. Some fences require a shortening of the stride in the middle, having already asked for a long one going in. The fence may then include another long stride going out if it is a multi-element fence.

If the fence is built to be jumped downhill, the horse is likely to gain a little extra ground through sheer momentum and this speed must be kept under control if things are not to get out of hand. Keep your legs on strongly to hold the horse together throughout. Do not get in front of the movement and keep your body fairly upright to maintain the balance. If the fence rides long, you must sit up but ride forward strongly, dictating the striding through the fence.

Water combinations are unique as they test the horse's courage as well as its athletic ability. The drag of the water creates another problem for the rider who must remain secure throughout as well as effective. If jumping a fence on dry land before dropping into water, the rider must be a little on the defensive in their position as getting too far forward before the inevitable drop into water can be the start of a series of mishaps. Always balance the horse by pushing it forward into a more contained outline and then keep this control until you are actually required to jump each fence.

Combinations come in numerous different forms and all require accurate, positive riding. Making the right initial decision for your horse is not always easy, so always have an alternative route in your mind in case things are not going too well or you have a problem at that particular fence.

Water combinations have an added hazard in that the spray created on jumping into the water can blur the rest of the fence. Keep the pace steady when going through water to ensure that you will still be able to see where to go.

Fences that incorporate double bounces require the maximum amount of spring and impulsion. Push the horse together between hand and leg and maintain this as you approach the fence. Your aim should be to release the power thus created in a controlled explosion over the fences. You must contain this power throughout so that the horse does not lose impulsion or spring as it negotiates each element. Accentuate your leg aids over each part and keep hold of the head.

Combinations going uphill obviously require extra impulsion, although this does not always mean speed. Always push the horse's hocks more underneath it as the fence is being approached and keep moving forward in a rhythm. Drive the horse on and up over each element, helping with your legs and keeping a forwards balance throughout.

Keeping to a line is normally vitally important in combinations if a successful outcome is to be achieved. However, it is important to be able to deviate from this if the horse's stride will bring it in too close or too far off, by knowing how to gain or lose a little ground when necessary. The speed of your approach and maintaining your line through the fence will both be helped by arriving at a good take-off spot. By standing off from the first element, you can gain a little more ground on the other side. By getting in close to the fence, you may be able to land a little further in and make the middle less of a stretch if the striding is long. You must, however, keep riding on strongly or maintain a strong feel on the reins to dictate what is needed throughout the obstacle.

Spreads

The spread fence is a particularly inviting fence when riding across country because the speed ridden at on such courses tends to increase the distance covered by the horse while in the air. Bearing in mind that the horse's average half-pace galloping stride is approximately 3.6 m (12 ft), it is easy to realize how this can increase dramatically in speed and impulsion through the air after take-off. My little 15 hh. Olympic horse, Our Nobby, supposedly jumped 8.2 m (27 ft) over a steeplechase fence when I was somewhat out of control during this phase and this is not exceptional by any means.

Generally speaking, it is best to jump a spread fence straight so that the width is kept to a minimum. If you angle the fence and/or come in rather close to it, the horse is more likely to touch the front with one front leg that is not yet fully tucked up. Some spreads are designed to be angled, however, such as footbridges, and your line of approach and accurate riding at such obstacles is most important.

Spread fences, such as parallels, sleeper stacks, tables, troughs, wagons, etc, are all fairly straightforward but do require accurate riding. Controlled impulsion at a sensible speed is what is needed. Arrive at your take-off spot in a good rhythm and let the fence come to you as you approach. Endless checking or overpushing only upsets the horse's rhythm and makes it impossible to maintain an even stride.

Do not push your horse into the bottom of a spread fence or it will be difficult to get the front end up in time. However, do not stand off too far away either, as this will force the horse to stretch. Should this happen, you must be ready to slip the reins as much as is required by the horse and keep the momentum going forward. At the same time, it is essential to stay in balance and not get left behind. This might cause your weight to come down on the saddle and make the horse hit the fence behind. Sometimes the result of this is for the horse to pitch forward, with the rider going unceremoniously over the ears!

This rider is travelling well and confidently over the spread and appears to have no worries.

Occasionally, a horse may put its feet down on a sleeper stack or table-type obstacle and the rider must be able to remain in balance when this happens. It is a rare occurrence but is a bit off-putting. There is little you can do except support the horse's front end on landing. Normally it will only have put its feet down to give itself a little more momentum.

It is not quite such good news when a horse puts its feet down on a hedge and then discovers, too late, that this is not as solid as it presumably thought! Self-preservation and strong survival instincts then take over. You will win some and lose others but, thankfully, this is a very rare mistake; it has probably only happened to me on about three or four occasions in the last 30 years.

Large parallels generally jump well but you must make sure your horse can see the back rail clearly to be able to gauge the size of its jump. By moving to the left or right a little, it is usually possible to make such a fence more inviting or obvious. Those that slope slightly in front are a little more forgiving than a square parallel, which requires accurate, positive riding.

A rail in front of a thick hedge looks more inviting but is much the same type of test. If there is a ditch in front, this almost acts as a guide to your take-off spot. Those with a ditch behind need riding at a little stronger to encourage the horse to jump out well.

Never come into a spread fence losing impulsion. This is the worst possible situation for the horse, which will then have to make a huge effort to clear the height and spread while lacking sufficient speed. If you are in doubt about your approach to this type of fence, the safest approach is to keep riding forward and keep hold of the head. The horse is quite capable of looking after itself if you give it the right help.

Uprights

An upright fence on a cross country course is generally straightforward but needs treating with care, especially if the siting of it is causing the fence to become more difficult. This is more likely to be the case in Intermediate and Advanced level courses than at the lower levels.

An upright on the flat may have a ground line in the form of a log, rails or ditch, which is helpful in assessing the take-off spot. For those that have no obvious ground line, you will need to set the horse up a little more in order to focus its eye on the fence. Some uprights are set going downhill and for these it is necessary to have the horse well balanced and back on its hocks so that it pops over without gaining too

Mark Todd demonstrates a beautifully balanced position over this obstacle –
soft hands, secure leg and looking towards the next fence.

much ground over the fence. The nearer you can get to the fence, the less likely you will be to jar the horse but you will need to be steady and under control at this type of obstacle. Sometimes approaching in a strong trot will be as easy as canter if the hill is quite steep.

Sometimes you will have two uprights to jump going downhill, one near the top and one near the bottom. The difficulty here is maintaining control for the second jump as the sheer momentum created after jumping the first tends to carry you towards the second a little on the fast side. Sit up, keep hold of the head and aim straight. Your reactions need to be fast in such situations so that you can quickly adjust, as necessary, to jumping one fence followed immediately by another. It is not unknown to find a third fence, but the same principle applies – sit up, keep hold of the head and aim straight.

Helsinki steps are sited on the side of a hill and these, often narrow, sections on different levels require accurate and positive riding. They may be very narrow, with several stepped sections, or less acute on a more gradual incline. Look at each section and its approach and decide which appears the most inviting to jump. The straighter you can jump the better but, because of their position on the side of a hill, it is not always easy to get the horse to approach them straight. Keep your legs on strongly and keep a firm hold to maintain your line towards the fence.

Any upright fence going uphill will need plenty of impulsion and your aim must be to get as close to the fence for take-off as possible. The further away you are, the higher the fence will become for the horse and so it will become a greater effort. Collect your horse together by pushing it into a stronger contact and maintain your rhythm towards the obstacle.

For uprights sited on the top of a hill, you must assess how puffed or tired your horse is going to be when it reaches the top, as even a superfit horse will become puffed if ridden too fast. The angle of degree of the hill and the length of the climb will affect different horses in different ways but your object must be to arrive at the top still able to negotiate the fence safely. Your angle of approach can make a big difference if you pull a little to the right or left and give the horse a few flat strides before reaching the fence. If at all possible, I try to avoid jumping a fence while still going uphill after a long pull. If there is no option, then really stoke the horse up, push it together, keep hold of its head and use your legs strongly to ensure that it has sufficient impulsion to jump clear.

Mistakes are often made at this type of fence because the rider does not push the horse together and help it enough to make this big effort after a tiring pull uphill. Keep your weight off the horse's back and help it to the top with sympathetic riding. Do not force or overtax it.

Water

When competing at higher levels the water jump becomes more of a feature fence than ever, with spectators crowding around in the hope of seeing someone receive a ducking. A drop into water is always quite daunting.

It is vital to get the speed of your approach right and to be in a steady rhythm. If you go in too slow, you will be liable to pitch forward on landing as your descent will have been very steep and you then risk unbalancing both of you. Going in too fast can be equally risky as you may overjump, and then not have sufficient balance and control to cope with both the drop and the drag of the water. If there is a fence in the water, or one on the way out, the horse is in danger of not seeing this at all because of the spray created by going in too fast.

You must be able to keep a balanced, forward approach that is right for your horse to be able to negotiate the fence with ease. You must go in neither too fast nor too slow but full of impulsion and control so that you will obtain the right reaction when required.

As soon as you are safely in, you should be able to sit up and steady the horse so that it can focus on how it is to come out. If there is a fence in the water, the horse must be allowed to see it properly. Steady the horse immediately you land in the water, to allow the spray to settle and the horse to see the obstacle, then keep hold of its head and ride it in a good rhythm towards this.

If there is a large expanse of water to go through, keep hold of the horse's head and keep it cantering steadily so that it maintains its balance and rhythm. If there is a step up or jump out, ensure that you allow the horse to focus on this before preparing to jump it.

All water fences need riding with controlled commitment: positive and forward but always in balance, with the rider maintaining a firm lower leg and allowing just enough rein to give the horse the freedom it requires.

Some fences have a bounce into water, which calls for an even more controlled approach but also stronger riding on the take-off to ensure that the momentum is maintained. A horse will normally back off a bounce a little to balance itself and you will need to be strong to keep up sufficient speed to prevent the horse from pitching forwards too much on landing in the water.

With alternative fences into water, it is often the case that you will have to turn rather sharply to negotiate the out part successfully. Be careful how you turn your horse as, if you are too sharp, it is easy to unbalance it and cause it to stumble. It is often best to pull up, turn round steadily and then set off again.

Banks and Steps

Banks and steps require a lot of impulsion, especially the uphill fences. For a big bank or a series of large steps, the horse should be pushed up together well and ridden really strongly up each step or on to a large bank. The secret with steps is to keep riding every step of the way and to keep your weight forward and in balance all the way to the top.

Coming down steps is much easier as the horse usually backs off and balances itself a little before jumping boldly downwards. Allow the reins far enough to give the horse freedom to jump but then support it a bit with a steady rein contact.

Karen Dixon and Get Smart sail off this big drop at Badminton in lovely style. She is supporting his head but still allowing enough rein for him to stretch out well.

RIDING THE SHOW JUMPING COURSE
AT A COMPETITION

Your show jumping round is likely to be extremely influential in your final placing. Mistakes here can prove extremely costly in a three-day event.

Warm your horse up well but don't overtire it at a three-day event as the speed and endurance sections will have taken quite a bit out of it. This would not apply at a one-day event.

Maintain a forward, flowing rhythm. Think about every stride as you approach your fences and save time wherever possible as the time is usually tight, particularly in three-day events. Keep the horse well balanced on turns and corners, and stick to your chosen lines round and through the fences. Maintain a strong lower leg and soft hands. Think forwards all the time.

The great Murphy Himself and Ian Stark en route *to a silver medal at the World Equestrian Games. This horse was a law unto himself, regularly defying all the rules of strides and distances and making daunting fences look ridiculously easy.*

*Check your tack, clothes and other necessary equipment before setting off.
Always take spares in case your tack breaks unexpectedly. A bridle is not
always the easiest item to borrow in an emergency!*

Check beforehand whether you should salute the judges or not and
what the start bell sounds like so that you are sure which signal is yours!
There is often a barrage of all sorts of noises at big events. Start as soon as
possible after the signal as only 30 seconds are allowed before you must
cross the start line.

Aim for that all-important clear round. This must be your first
priority. If you experience difficulties in your show jumping, you should
seek the necessary help to perfect your technique in this phase.

GENERAL TIPS AT COMPETITIONS

Whatever course you are riding, be positive, ride steadily and in a rhythm that is right for your horse, the ground conditions and your aim for the day.

1 Give yourself time to do everything properly so that your horse is given the best chance, whether in dressage, show jumping or cross country.

2 Check everything carefully before you set off and be professional in your approach. This goes for your leg protection, first aid for horse and rider, the condition of all tack, riding clothes, hay and food, grooming kit, stud kit, mucking-out kit, etc.

3 Know when everything is happening and write out a plan for your helpers so that everyone is aware of what is happening and when.

4 Brief your helpers on what you want and how you want things done and when. Communication is the name of the game!

5 Do not forget to inform your owners/sponsors of times and directions to the event. Send or leave car passes etc for them. Make sure someone is going to look after them so that they have a good day out.

6 Learn your dressage test thoroughly – it's a maddening way to lose unnecessary marks.

7 Check the lorry or trailer thoroughly, including tyres and lights, and fill up with fuel. Check water, oil and windscreen washer fluid.

8 Write out your route to the event and know how long you expect the journey to take.

9 Provided you are *not* doing the driving, spend some time on the journey thinking about your chosen route round the course and what you are planning to achieve.

10 Go out to enjoy yourself and give your horse the best possible chance. Learn from any mistakes you make and ensure that they do not happen again.

INDEX

Page numbers in *italic* refer to illustrations.

Advanced competitions 79, 129, 146, 150, 167
angled fences 101–2
arrowheads 104, 156
azoturia 138

Badminton 27, *106, 107, 109*, 146, *160, 171*
balance 84, 153
bandages 33, 38, 140
banks *114–15*, 114–18, *116–17*, 170–1
Barcelona Olympics *67, 110*
barley 41
Beavan, Lynne *107*
bends 62
bits 46–8, 98–9
Bliss, Nancy *94*
Blocker, Herbert *67*
boots (horses) 32–3, 83, 140
bounces 89, *90*, 104, *113*, 114, 156, 164, 170
    double 16, 104, 164
bridles 144
bullfinches 121–2
Burghley *66, 109, 112*

Campbell, Nicholas *111*
cantering 27, *28*, 57–8, *59*, 61, 62, 77, 78, 92–3
    speeds 78, *81*, 81, 129–30
    through poles 89
chambon, lungeing in a 52
Cleverly, Tanya *66*
clipping 44
coffins 16, 121, 125–7, *126–7*
collected canter *59*, 74
collection 58, 60–1
combination fences 24, *70–1, 136–7, 160, 162*, 162–5, *163*
conformation 8, 9–13, *10*, 27

back *10*, 11, 20, *21*
ears and eyes 9
feet 8, *11, 12*, 13
head 9–10
and jumping ability 20–1
limbs 8, 9, 11–13
neck 10
quarters *10*, 11, 20, *21*
shoulders 10, 20, *21*
tail 11
withers 10
cool-down period 74, *76*, 77
corner fences 102–3, *103*, 156, *156–7*
counter-canter 62, 74
cross country (phase D) 92–3
    competing at events 146, *148*, 155–71
    distances, times and speeds 130, 158, 159
    jumping techniques 99–127
    pre-season schooling round 72
cubbing 15
curb bits 47

Davidson, Bruce *108, 112*
de Gogue, riding in a *52*, 52
distances 129–32, 158–9
Dixon, Karen 171
dressage 31, *66*, 81, 145, 146–7, 174

early events 16–17, *17*

fast work 128–32
fences
    combination 24, *70–1, 136–7, 160, 162*, 162–5, *163*
    cross-country 99–127, *100*, 155–71
    going downhill *70–1*, 167–8
    going uphill 118, 165, 170
    grid work 68, 89–92, *90, 91*
    jumping a course *94*, 94–8, *95, 97*

'rider frighteners' *111*
steeplechase 99
fitness programmes 54–64, 73–84, 132
    personal 18–20, *19*
flat banks *116–17*, 118
flat work 56, 58, *66*, 128
flying change 93
forehand, turns on the 62, *63*

gadgets 50–3, *51, 52, 53*
gags 46–7, 47–8, 98–9
galloping 27, 30, 79, 128–9, 149
Gatcombe *65*, 120
girths 144
Grakle nosebands 47, *57*
grid work 68, 89–92, *90, 91*
ground conditions 15, 37, 99, 129, 131, 132–4

hackamores 49–50, *50*
hacking 30, 85, 116, 132
half-circles 61
half coffins 125
half-halts 31, 56, 59, 61, 74
half-pass *63, 73*, 74
halts 56, 59–60
haunches, turns on the 62, *63*
helpers 151, 174
Helsinki steps 169
horses
    drinking water 137, 139, 142
    feeding 40–2, *42*
    footcare 33–8, *34*
    fresh air *44*, 44–5
    jumping ability 21, 22, 22–4, *24*
    leg care/protection 8, *32*, 32–3, 38–40, *39, 40*, 48, 151
    cold hosing 38, *39*
    mental health 45–6
    muscular structure 20–4, *21*
    one-sided *48*, 48
    paces 27–30, *28, 29*
    preventing heatstroke and dehydration 135–9, 142

reflexes 22, 23, 24
retraining 53
sensitive 15, 46
shoeing 8, 33–5, *34*, *141*, 141–2
spooky 96, *123*
stabling 44–6, *45*
temperament 8, 13–15, *14*, 21, 25–6, *26*
toothcare 43, 48
washing down 138, 139, 151
worming 43–4
young eventers 15–16
see also conformation
hunter trials 15

impulsion 58, 167, 169, 170
Intermediate competitions 16, 79, 146, 167
interval training 55, 77, 78, 80–3, *81*, *82*, 128

lateral work 62
Latta, Vicky *65*
leg-yielding 56, *63*, *64*, 64
Leng, Ginny *109*
loops 62, 74

maize 41
martingales 47
Moore, Owen *105*

Normandy banks *114–15*, 118
Norman, Sarah *112*
nosebands 47
Novice competitions 16, 20, 146, 150
fitness programmes 54, 79
numnahs 140, 142

oats 41
one-day events 16, 129, 145–6, 172
fitness programme for 79
overhangs, jumping through 125

parallels (spread fences) 165, 167
Parsonage, Gary *105*
Phase A (roads and tracks) 130, 146, 147–9, *148*

phase B *see* steeplechase (phase B)
Phase C (roads and tracks) 130, *148*, 149–51
phase D *see* cross country
poles
exercises 85–9, *86*, *87*, *88*
grid work *90*, 90, *91*, 92
zig-zags 125
Pre-Novice competitions 16, 129

reins
bridging *142–3*, 144
running 50, *51*
rhythm 27, *84*, 84, 131, 151, 153, 172, 174
riders
body weight 92
equipment *150*, *174*
and the horse's jumping ability 23–4, *24*
and the horse's temperament 25–6, *26*
mental approach 8, 17–18, 151, 159
physical preparation 18–20, *19*
roads and tracks (phases A and C) 68, 146, 147–52, 158, 159
rugging 44
Ryan, Matt *67*, *109*

schooling *57*, 57–74, *59*
aids 50–3, *51*, *52*, *53*
shoeing 8, 33–5, *34*, *141*, 141–2, 151
shoulder-in 30, 56, 62, *63*, *73*, 73–4
show jumping 94–8, *95*, *97*
competition courses 172, *172–3*, *173*
slow work 55–6
speeds 78, *81*, 81, *82*, 129–30
roads and tracks 147–9
three day events 158–9
spread fences 89, 91, *100*, 101, 156, 165–7, *166*
stable management 8, 31–53
stables, location of 46
Stark, Ian *100*, *106*, *144*, 172
start boxes 149, 151–2, 153

steeplechase (phase B) 98–9
distances, times and speeds 83, 130, 131, 158, 159
riding the course 146, 147, *148*, 149, *152*, 152–5
training 98–9
steps 114–18, 170–1
straightness 60
studs *35*, 35–8, *36*, *133*, 133

tack 46–53, 140, *144*, 144, *173*
choosing 46–53, 138, 151
Tait, Blyth *107*
team chases *17*, 83
Thomson, Mary *106*
three-day events 146, 172
distances, times and speeds 129–32, 158–9
fitness programmes 54, 55, 79, 132
thrush 38
tiger traps 121
timing 99, 151, 153, 158–9
interval training *81*, 81–3
Todd, Mark *119*, *168*
trakehners 121, 122, *123*, *154–5*
trotting *28*, 56, 89
turns, on the forehand and haunches 62, *63*
two-day events 146

upright fences 89, 90, 101, 156, 167–9, *168*, 169

Walker, Richard *110*
warm-up period 74–7, *75*
water jumps 72, 96, *97*, *111*, *112*, 131
cross-country courses 118–21, *119*, *120*, 160, 169–70
combinations 163, *164*
weather conditions 135–9, *139*
weight carried *140*, 140–1
Wheeler, Natasha 69
World Equestrian Games *172*

zig-zags *124*, 124–5